John Murray
Aberdeen
October 1985

PROPHET AND PRIEST
IN OLD ISRAEL

PROPHET AND PRIEST IN OLD ISRAEL

ADAM C. WELCH, D.D.

EMERITUS PROFESSOR OF HEBREW AND OLD TESTAMENT EXEGESIS
NEW COLLEGE, EDINBURGH

Author of
The Code of Deuteronomy, Post-Exilic Judaism
etc.

STUDENT CHRISTIAN MOVEMENT PRESS
58 BLOOMSBURY STREET, LONDON, W.C.1

First published May 1936

Printed in Great Britain

PREFACE

THIS study of an old theme in Old Testament religion is based on two convictions. On the one side is a strong sense of the extent to which the Hebrew faith has deepened and enriched the worship of men. Its cult not only kept Judaism together after the debacle of the Exile : it has contributed rich and enduring elements to the religious practice of Christendom. The Evangelical Church has given high place to the ethical message of the prophets, and has spared no labour in order to make clear the meaning and the scope of that message. But it has not always acknowledged the extent of its debt to the older faith in connection with its worship. Yet one need only recall the use it has made of the Psalter, the prayer-book of the second temple, in order to realise how deeply the older cult has influenced its thought on the relation between the soul and God. On the other hand, the prophets did not criticise from the outside a religion in which they did not share. They sprang from Israel, and, as they could not have

existed in any other nation, they could not have
found an audience in any other nation. However violent their criticism of the national religion was, it came from men who had been
reared in it, and was therefore fruitful. The
purpose of the present discussion has been to
sketch how much they effected rather than the
extent of their failure.

The author's sense of the hurrying foot of
time has prevented him from developing the
subject with the fulness which it deserves. To
mention only one cognate theme, Professor Alt
has recently pointed out that certain laws in the
Book of the Covenant bear evidence of having
been derived from a source external to Israel.
It is well known that the legislation of Deuteronomy and Leviticus is partly based on the Book
of the Covenant and has developed those earlier
laws. It would be possible, in the light of Alt's
suggestion, to compare, *e.g.* the laws in Deuteronomy which are similar to those in the earlier
code, and to show that Israel adapted legislation
which was neutral in its character to conform
with its own genius. The prophetic ideals,
which remoulded the original cult, were at work
on the social legislation. But the author must
be content to suggest the lines along which a
new approach may be made to a large question,

and he may venture to express the hope that younger students, even some of his former pupils, may carry on, correct, and supplement what he has begun.

Meantime he acknowledges the help he has received from one of those former students, Mr David M. G. Stalker, M.A., who has corrected the proofs of this book and has prepared the index.

ADAM C. WELCH

EDINBURGH

CONTENTS

PROPHET AND PRIEST
IN OLD ISRAEL

I

THE QUESTION AT ISSUE

IT is always difficult to discover a title which will adequately define the scope and describe the purpose of a special study in the religious life of Israel. There may, therefore, be a certain advantage in stating that the preparation of the Baird Lecture on Post-Exilic Judaism forced on the author's attention certain questions as to the character of the worship of Israel. Judaism after the Return reconstituted itself round the temple and the sacrificial system. The recognition of this fact drove a student to attempt to determine the place of this cult in the nation's religious life before the Return, and to define the relation of the prophets, the other factor in Israel's religion, to its cult. Was the new Judaism, which appeared after the Exile, a legitimate development from the national past, or was it a deliberate return to an earlier attitude to the cult?

What makes the question more difficult and more urgent is that an influential school of Old

Testament scholars believe the Hebrew cult to
have been no native product, but to have been
mainly or even wholly taken over from the
Canaanites after the invading Israelites had
settled in Palestine. This school believes that
the high places, which occupy a large space in
the records preceding the Exile but which disappeared after the Return, were originally places
of native worship and were adopted by the new-
comers. The stories which relate that Abraham,
Isaac, and Jacob built altars and offered sacrifice
at certain sanctuaries in Palestine are no more
than an attempt, as it were, to sprinkle holy
water on these shrines, and to obscure the fact
that they were originally of pagan origin. Along
with the sacred places the Israelites adopted
the sacred emblems associated with them, and
made use especially of the מצבה or standing-
stone and the אשרה or pole consecrated to a
goddess. They further took over the ritual
which was practised at these places, and in particular they accepted the annual festivals with
the custom of pilgrimage to the leading shrines.
The obvious connection between these festivals,
which became a prominent feature in the cult,
and the agricultural seasons is considered to
prove that they must have been borrowed by
the invaders. Men who had arrived from the

desert and who for at least a generation had
been nomads there, could not have evolved
practices of worship which clearly bear the
stamp of the settled life. Finally, the conquerors adopted from the conquered the sacrificial ritual which attended both the communal festivals and the private sacrifices of
individuals.

Accordingly Dr Robinson of Cardiff finds
himself able to make the following general
statement on the subject : " It seems, in fact,
that they (*i.e.* the Israelites) simply adopted the
culture of Palestine *en bloc*. Just as the Teutonic
invaders of the fourth century A.D. adapted
themselves in large measure to the culture of
Imperial Rome, so these new conquerors of
Palestine inherited with the land they occupied
much, if not all, of the existing mode of life.
And to carry the parallel a step further, just as
the northern invaders of the ancient Mediter-
ranean world accepted in the main the religion
of the land which they entered, so too the
Israelites went far in accepting the deities and
the cultus which they found already in the
country. For some generations we must expect to find little difference, if any, between
the faith of the older inhabitants and that of
the new-comers. In addition to the natural

respect which even a victorious race feels for the higher culture of its defeated enemy, there were strong reasons which predisposed the new-comers to adopt the cultus and belief of their predecessors." [1]

This view of the origin of the cult is closely associated with the opinion held as to the attitude of the prophets to the sacrificial system. Those religious teachers, as is generally recognised, criticised with great severity the popular worship of their time, and spoke with vehemence alike about the priests who conducted it and about the worshippers who took part in it. It has long been a question whether their strong language on the subject involved a demand for the purification of the cult, a different estimate of its place in the religious life of their nation, or a condemnation of the entire system *per se*. In their work of reform the prophets may have criticised one feature or another in the popular cult, but may have aimed at retaining it in a purer form. Or they may have rebuked the undue devotion of the common people to out-ward forms of devotion in contrast with their indifference to the claims of God on their moral obedience. The opinion which this school holds on the origin and character of the Hebrew cult

[1] *Hebrew Religion*, pp. 169 f.

inevitably drives them to a more extreme estimate of the prophetic attitude.   According to
them the prophets, recognising the sacrificial
system to have been pagan in its origin, saw
also that it embodied a wholly alien conception of the character of the God of Israel, as
well as of the relation which He held to the
elect nation.   They therefore demanded, with
more or less clearness, its abolition, as false in
its source and mischievous in its effects.   Their
polemic was directed against the sacrificial
system *per se*.

Now these two positions, which are thus
essentially allied, are open to grave objection
from the side of their interpretation of the
facts which appear in the documents.   Thus
Dr Robinson's analogy between the Hebrew
invasion of Palestine and the victory of the
northern nations in the fourth century A.D. is
too vague, too distant in time, and especially too
unlike in character to be other than misleading.
The Old Testament documents present us with
the picture of a group of clans which were
welded together by a common religion and which
carried out their wars of conquest in the name
of their national God.   Their wars were holy
wars, and the men who took part in them
claimed to be following divine prompting and

to be under divine guidance. The northern
invasion bore no such character, but was more
like the spilling over of a swollen reservoir. It
was as natural for these new-comers to borrow
from the civilisation they overturned its methods
and its ideals, as it was to loot its property.
There is a much closer analogy between the
Hebrew invasion of Canaan and the early vic-
tories of Islam, since both were carried out
under the influence of religion : and, as their
impulse was the same, their first effect was the
same. In its early enthusiasm Islam wrecked the
older civilisations, and set up an austere puritan-
ism in their place : in Palestine the excavations
prove the conquest to have resulted in a sudden
collapse of certain outward signs of a higher
civilisation, and the Hebrew documents at least
witness to the emergence of a nation devoted
to its own God. The evidence we possess
points to a violent change rather than a gradual
absorption. Again, it is a mere assumption to
state that the Hebrew high places were originally pagan sanctuaries and that the idea of them
having owed their origin to the patriarchs was
intended to conceal this fact. For the majority
of the shrines where the patriarchs are said to
have offered sacrifice have no association with
the later worship. On the other hand, the

spade has discovered two older sanctuaries at Gezer and Taanach. These, as would naturally be expected with an agricultural people, were not placed on the hills, but in low-lying territory; and neither of these ever became a cult-centre for Israel. Finally, the judgment that the prophets were unanimous in their attitude toward the cult, and that they agreed in condemning it *per se*, does not do justice to the facts. For it ignores that such prophets as Samuel, Elisha, and even Elijah appeared in close association with the altars, and were even represented as having taken part in the worship there. Men like Samuel who presided over the sacrificial feast at a village high place (1 Sam. ix. 15 ff.), or like Elijah who said he had been very jealous for the Lord, because the children of Israel had thrown down the Yahweh altars (1 Kings xix. 14), or like Elisha about whom a man at Shunem thought it natural that his wife should go to consult the prophet at new moon or Sabbath, were certainly not opposed to the cult on principle. As for the oracles of the later prophets, it cannot be proved that they all took the same attitude on that question or on other questions. That they did so and that their common view was one which condemned the cult *in toto* can only be proved from isolated

B

passages pressed beyond the terms of a just exegesis. The subject would not have been so long and seriously discussed, if its decision had been as sure as is sometimes claimed.

The reader of the following discussion is not invited to travel again along this well-trodden highway. The only reason for touching on the matter at all has been to enter a caveat against the large and sometimes airy generalities which frequently appear in connection with the subject. These are apt to mislead, since they leave the impression that there can be only one reasonable view as to the origin and character of the Hebrew cult, or as to the prophetic attitude toward it. It is necessary to emphasise that these general statements cannot claim to be anything more than working hypotheses, which have been framed to account for certain undoubted facts, but which must never through carelessness or forgetfulness slip into the position of holding a right to any higher authority.

The purpose here is to approach the whole question from a different angle—the angle of one who has for some years devoted a good deal of attention to the Judaism which emerged after the Exile and which largely determined the bent of Jewish life and religion since that time. The conclusions which were the result of that study have been published, but they differ too widely from received opinion on the period to be called in evidence. There are, however, certain features of the post-exilic movement which are patent even to those who have not devoted special attention to it. Thus, at a peculiarly critical stage in its national history, when it seemed possible that its life as a people might disappear, Israel rallied on its cult. The temple and the sacrificial system practised there became its centre as they had never before been, because these represented what was peculiarly its own. Israel had lost its kingdom and its independence, and with these control over the outward forms of its life. All that was left to it of its distinctive life was its religion, and the element in its religion which it elected for its centre was its cult. As is always the case where a people reacts against anything which threatens its national identity and its peculiar genius, the movement was strongly, even stubbornly, conservative in its character. Over against the heathenism which was threatening to engulf it and to swallow up its native life, as it had already swallowed up its independence, Israel flung back upon its past, because it found there some guarantee for the preservation of what was

representative of its character.[1] Now, when
the people restored what thus represented their
peculiar life in the past, they renewed the temple
and the sacrificial system at Jerusalem. Evidently they recognised in their cult something
which was distinctively their own.

But this significant feature in their history
involves two conclusions which have a bearing
on the present inquiry. Since Israel rallied on
its cult at this particular time, the people must
have recognised in it something which was so
peculiar to itself that it served to mark them
off from the heathen world among which they
must live. What makes this more noteworthy
is that it did have that effect. For it is generally
acknowledged that from the time of the Return
the Jew came to stand aloof from his world in
a new way. Whereas he had up to this period
been prepared to assimilate much from his
neighbours, to intermarry with them, to enter
into foreign alliances, to borrow freely even
foreign workmen for so intimate a service as

[1] I write as a Scot, member of a little people which has
always been conscious of its neighbourhood to a predominant
partner. We, better than most, recognise the reason which
led one of our own people, Lady John Scott, to bid us " haud
fast by the past." We know, too, the reason which makes
many of our kin maintain habits and idioms, though they
smile at themselves even while they maintain these.

the building of the temple, he now drew apart into a life of his own. This jealous separation from the heathen environment among which Israel now lived coincided in time with the movement by which the people constituted itself on the basis of its religion : its aim was both national and religious. But it grew stronger after the restoration of the temple, when the people, alike in Palestine and in the diaspora, accepted the sacrificial system there as valid for and obligatory on every Jew. The network of regulations as to food and as to ceremonial purity were the characteristic features of Jewish life which marked off every Jew from his neighbour. But the purpose of these regulations was to preserve in all the members of the race the condition of purity which made them fit to take part in the sacrificial worship. The separation of the Jew from his world not only coincided in time with the restoration of the temple-worship, but was the direct result of this cult. In view of this it becomes extremely difficult to believe that the cult on which the men rallied, and which had this for its result, had originally been no integral part of their peculiar religion, but had been borrowed wholesale from the very paganism against which they were now reacting. In that case they found their support

in asserting their peculiar character as a people
from a system which was not native to their
own life.

Another conclusion, however, results from the
situation after the Return. The people found
their centre and renewed their life on the sacrificial
system. If now the whole body of the prophets
had united in condemning that system as pagan
in its origin and alien in its character to the true
faith, this can only mean that post-exilic Judaism
deliberately turned its back on the prophets
and rejected their distinctive teaching. Kuenen
recognised the difficulty which this presented to
his view of the course of events in the pre-
exilic period. He therefore attempted to con-
nect the work of the returned exiles with the
teaching of the prophets. According to him the
prophets had succeeded in lodging in the minds
of the people that their misfortunes, especially
the crowning catastrophe of the Exile, were due
to their sins. When, therefore, this disaster
befell the men, they turned to their priests and
asked for guidance as to how they might prevent
the recurrence of such a penalty. In answer to
this the priests produced their torah with the
assurance that strict obedience to its terms would
guarantee the divine favour. The theory is
naïvely artificial in its terms. It requires us to

believe that Jewry, which by this time was scattered in Palestine, Babylonia, and Egypt, was sufficiently homogeneous to reach one mind and could find a central authority with power to answer its doubts or to enforce a decision. No great movement in religious history ever took its source from such a deft arrangement. It is a more grave objection, however, to notice that the supposed explanation evades the real question. The sins against which the prophets protested, and which according to them had resulted in the punishment of the exile, were sins against the moral demands of their God. According to Kuenen, these men had protested against the nation's devotion to the cult because this devotion had led to neglect of the weightier matters of the law. It could not therefore have been the prophetic message with its supposed verification in history which drove the people into a blindfold obedience to their priests. For the prevailing characteristic of the new polity was that it gave a central place to the very system which the prophets had condemned. Yet Kuenen's theory had and has one great merit : the great Dutch scholar recognised the necessity for linking up the prophetic movement with the later polity which made the cult the dominant element in the life of Israel. Otherwise there was no real continuity in the nation's religious history.

Unless some vital connection can be made between prophetism and post-exilic Judaism, the consequence must be to make the prophetic testimony a mere interlude in the religious history of the nation. While the men lived, they were unable to effect their purpose of dislodging the cult from its place in the reverence of their people. In the end Israel ignored their teaching and constituted itself round an institution which was borrowed from paganism and instinct with that spirit. This can only mean that the prophetic contribution is wholly isolated in the life of the nation out of which it came. It had no roots in the religious life of its people, since it was rather a strong criticism of and protest against the practices of that religious life. It passed without effecting much, for the people reverted at last to the practices against which the protest had been directed, and constituted itself round a cult which the prophets had unanimously and unhesitatingly condemned.

Apart from every other consideration, such an interpretation of its history fails to explain the survival of Israel. The nation had ceased to possess any of the outward forms which had hitherto marked it off from its world. Yet, at the very time when the other little peoples were being absorbed into a larger Empire, Israel not only continued Israel, but became more sharply distinct than before. It must have done this through the reassertion of elements in its life which were peculiar to itself. The more scholars insist on the essential likeness between Israel's forms of worship and those of its neighbours, the more hopeless does it become to explain this fact of history. The other cults vanished underground, as soon as the nations which practised them lost their identity. Their later influence was wholly indirect and obscure. Since they possessed no distinctive character of their own, they could not maintain the separate life of the peoples which practised them. A cult which became the rallying-point to prevent Israel from disappearing in the melting-pot must have possessed some quality of its own. Regarded merely from the point of view of history, the cult of Israel must have been fundamentally different from the rest in order to produce such different results.

But further, post-exilic Judaism did more than hold together the scattered people who acknowledged the authority of Jerusalem. It gave them a certain inspiration which made the

Jew an influence and a moral and spiritual
ferment in every land to which his wandering
feet led him. What seems to have attracted
attention, and even proselytes, was the Jewish
monotheism and the higher morale of the
people, so that, behind the singular cult and its
ceremonial demands, men must have been able
to recognise the presence of a nobler spirit. In
time the religion became the seed-bed of the
Christian Church, and it is impossible to read the
New Testament without noting the extent to
which our Lord and His apostles made use of
the worship which was practised at the temple.
He resorted to the festivals there, and after His
Passion they continued to go up to its courts
for prayer. Even when the infant Church left
Jerusalem they carried with them much which
could serve their purpose. Thus they made the
Holy Scripture of Judaism their own Canon,
but inside this they did not find it necessary to
make any distinction. They set on the same
level the oracles of the prophets, the histories,
the sacrificial law, the words of the sages. They
interpreted the life of their Master in the light
of the older Jewish Messiah, and construed
His Passion along the lines of the sacrificial
system. In particular they carried with them the
Psalter, which has been frequently described as

the hymn-book of the second temple. A more adequate title would be that of the Jewish prayer-book, for this name would better describe its contents and would also serve to explain the place it won not only in the temple, but in the synagogue. Opinion differs very widely as to the date and the purpose of the individual psalms, but it is commonly agreed that the book was brought into its present form by the authorities at the second temple, and that it was largely employed in connection with the worship there. It is a product of post-exilic Judaism, and, like everything else in that movement, was intended to serve the cult. It passed into the use of the synagogues all over the world, and formed the background of their prayers. This Psalter in its entirety became an abiding part of Christian worship, so that to this day its contents are recited year by year in Jewish synagogues, and in Roman Catholic and Anglican churches. Even those communions which do not employ it in its completeness or in its original form owe more than they always realise to its influence. Its language and its spirit have passed into and have profoundly determined the temper of Christian devotion. The fact deserves more attention than it has generally received. An undue stress has been laid by many evangelical

Churches and Christians on the value of the ethical teaching of the prophets, until it has almost come to be supposed that this is the only element which we owe to the Old Testament. The result has been to make men forget another debt of at least equal moment. It is the Jew who has taught the world to pray, and the Christian world is still praying in the temper, even in the terms which it has learned from the older faith. But prayer is in itself essentially a cult-act, since it is a means by which men maintain their relation to God. The prayer-book also of which all Christians make such constant use was closely associated with the sacrificial system, and was collected by a Judaism which had constituted itself round the temple. It is impossible to believe that a cult, which could make use of those noble and enduring prayers, was essentially pagan in its origin and wholly alien to the prophetic view of the relation between Israel and its God.

That is a brief and somewhat incomplete statement of the question which has pressed itself on the attention of one who in recent years has tried to work out the earlier question of the reconstitution of Israel after the Return. It became abundantly clear that the movement was strongly conservative in its attitude, and that the men were aiming at the restoration of their old means of grace. It was equally clear that the new Judaism was based on the temple and the cult there. If then the cult was an element in the life of Israel which it had borrowed from the Canaanites, and which the representatives of the Mosaic tradition had always and absolutely condemned, this seemed to imply that the nation rallied on something which was not representative of their peculiar outlook and native genius. Yet, when they did this, they not only succeeded in maintaining themselves, but contributed something of permanent value to a religion which was ethical and spiritual in its character.

In attempting a more satisfying account of the place which the cult occupied in the early life of Israel and of the relation of the prophets to it, I acknowledge the preconception, or, if the other word be preferred, the bias with which I approach the subject. This arises from the fact that, before being appointed to teach Hebrew, I spent more than twenty happy years as minister of a congregation. The duty involved in such work does not admit of a man devoting his whole time to Hebrew study, but it has certain compensations in helping him to understand the Old Testament. For it enables

him to learn what religion actually is and how
it functions in the life of a community. He
cannot fail to discover that a living religion is
not merely a set of ideas, more or less self-
consistent, more or less capable of being correlated into a system. A professor, who has
passed from being a student into a chair and
who has spent his life in lecturing, enormously
overrates the value of ideas expressed in words.
He himself spends most of his life among
words, which to him are the final expression of
ideas. But the minister of a congregation soon
discovers that religion, when it passes into the
lives of men, is expressed, not in men's words,
but in the things they do day by day in consequence of their faith. The attendance of
Christian men on divine service, their setting
apart one day in seven, not as a mere relaxation
from work, but as a means of maintaining the
life of their souls, their observance of Holy
Communion, their practice of prayer with the
submission of this practice to some rules are
matters which one who deals in words and systems
is inclined to dismiss as forms, even as accretions
to religion. In reality these constitute an acting
religion, and are as essential elements in its life
as the words which are forms to embody ideas.
Religion consists in what men do because of

what they believe, and their acts are as vital as their creeds. The word must take flesh and tabernacle among men in acts of piety before it can become a religion. The ideas men hold of their god, of their relation to him, of the right way to approach him, of the means to maintain this relation while it exists, of the means to restore it should it have been broken must translate themselves into acts of worship which may take the form of words of adoration or of petition to their god, or which may appear as sacrificial rituals or sacraments. These form the cult which at once embodies and maintains the religious life. But these acts of faith, which a man would never have performed except at the bidding of his faith, are no mere formalities or insignificant accretions which gather round the sublimated essence of this faith and may be ignored. They constitute an active religion, and without them the religion of a community or nation cannot exist.

Accordingly, while it is legitimate to speak about the teaching or the ideals or the convictions of the prophets, it is simply a misnomer to speak of their religion. None of those great men ever professed his intention to found a religion. Even Jeremiah who came nearest to such a position, when he counselled the exiles

in Babylonia to practise the presence of God by
prayer in the new conditions to which He had
brought them, did not attempt such a thing.
For he did not invent prayer, nor did he write
as though the exiles were to begin an act which
they had never before practised. What he did
was to insist on the magnitude and the power
of that practice in their cult which could never
be taken from them, and which was of such
significance that it could fill the place of all
that they had lost in their present season of
distress. They could maintain their relation to
their God through the simplest ritual of their
religion, but they must maintain a relation to
their God, and, in order to do this, must
maintain certain acts of faith.

Again, it was a constant burden of the prophets to urge upon their people the necessity
for practising righteousness and mercy in all
their relations to one another. But they never
presented these excellent virtues as though they
in themselves constituted the whole content of
Israel's religion, any more than they constituted
the entire relation between Israelite and Israelite.
The national life was the quick and varied
pattern of human life in every generation, where
men bought and sold, married wives and set up
homes, lived as masters and servants, united for

business and for merriment. To fulfil life they built themselves villages and towns, and set up councils to govern their behaviour, law courts to compose their quarrels. These relations were there, as they have always been : but, said the prophets, unless the foundation was laid in righteousness and mercy, and unless the loose structure was cemented by the same essential elements, they were not those which belonged to Israel. These great principles were the norm for a true Israel. And these essential factors in Israelite life, according to the prophetic teaching, derived directly from God. They were part of the revelation which He had made to the nation which He had chosen. The right of the prophet to insist upon them derived from the fact of his own intimate relation to the same God, and of his being a member of Israel. God had brought Israel into a peculiar relation to Himself and had made it the sphere of His self-revelation. He had made known that righteousness and mercy belonged to His nature and that without these it was impossible to please Him. But these commanding virtues did not constitute the relation between Israel and its God any more than they constituted the relation between fellow-Israelites. The relation was one which God had instituted in order that the

c

divine life might be transmitted for the help, the guidance, and, when the need emerged, the forgiveness of the nation. Acts of faith on the part of the people were needed, acts which the people would not have performed but for their trust in their God, in order to maintain their sense of their relation to Him. The norm for all such acts must be the same norm which governed the relations between Israelites, the revealed character of their God.

The function of the prophet was to maintain the standard which must determine the life of the nation, alike in its conduct and in its worship. Hence the men were integrally related to the religion of their people, and were no isolated phenomena in the course of Israel's history and faith. They sprang from the loins of their nation and were conscious of sharing its peculiar genius. They were proud of the common heritage and recalled the great past which had served to make Israel what it was. Their oracles are so closely related both to the past of the people and to its actual condition that they cannot be fully understood when they are separated from the peculiarly national life. Those living words lose half their force when they are torn away from the circumstances in which they were spoken and from the conditions to which they were addressed. In these oracles the men dealt out sharp judgment both on the moral condition of their people and on the practices by which they were seeking to maintain and to ensure the favour of God. Whether they dealt with moral questions or with the cult, they based their judgments on the character of God ; but the God in whose name they spoke, and whose condemnation of the nation they anticipated, was one whom Israel also acknowledged and, however mistakenly, was seeking to serve through its public acts of worship. Hence prophet and people had their roots in a common past, the traditions of which belonged to them both. The prophet censured in his own nation what he would never have blamed in another people, because they alone possessed the norm which he applied to their conduct. The relations which existed between fellow-Israelites and the cult by which they sought to maintain their relation to their God were not in agreement with the conception of His nature and will which He had made known to them alone. Nor were they helping men to realise the character of Him who had made them a peculiar people by making them His own.

But the prophets never sought to found a

new cult, any more than they attempted to create a new nation. In both cases they would serve Israel, which owed its being to an act of God, by making every form of its life worthy of its high vocation.

II

ISRAEL'S EARLY CULT AND THE
MOSAIC REFORM

IT is useful, and for the present purpose even
necessary, to go back to the period before
Israel arrived in Palestine, and to inquire how
much is known about the character of the
people's religion before the Exodus. For the
clans, which came under the influence of the
Mosaic reform and which were by this welded
into a federation so that they became the back-
bone of the later nation, were not destitute of
religious practices when they went down into
Egypt. The Old Testament writers recognised
this when they ascribed certain convictions and
certain outward observances to the early patriarchs : they also recognised that these differed
materially from those of their own time. It is
impossible to accept the picture they have given
of that religion, for the men transformed the life
of their forefathers to an extent which has made
it ideal, not actual. Nor are there any sure
criteria which make it possible to determine
what distinguished that early faith from those
of the other nations : it is even impossible to
pronounce with certainty that there was any

essential distinction. The greater probability is that the practices of that period closely resembled those of the Semitic world of which the men formed a part. The recent discoveries at Ras Shamra, though their evidence has not yet been thoroughly sifted, bear out this conclusion, for they show a striking resemblance to the cult of later Israel in certain forms of sacrifice and in the words which were applied to these.

The mere transference of the clans to Egypt cannot have produced much change in this respect, since the men were relegated to a district near the frontier, where they were able to continue their old manner of life. In particular, they maintained some features of their cult, for the narrative shows them to have been conscious of the difference between their native forms of worship and those of the Egyptians.[1] Since these derived from their former nomadic life and resembled in general those of their Semitic environment, they were less liable to be influenced by the rituals peculiar to Egypt.

That this is no generality based on mere supposition is proved from what is known about the religion of the Hebrews at the time. Thus Passover is universally recognised to have been a ritual observance native to the people, which

[1] Gen. xliii. 32 ; Exod. viii. 25-28.

was practised by them before the settlement in Canaan. The sources which refer so much of the sacrificial system to the stay at Horeb, uniformly describe Passover as having been in active use before the Exodus. Since in its early form it was a family rite, where the house-father acted as priest and where no altar was needed, there was no difficulty in maintaining it during the stay in Goshen. This character attached to the rite always, for, while the locus was shifted to the sanctuary and the actual slaying of the victim, with the manipulation of the blood, was carried out by the priests, the essential features of the rite remained in the homes of the people. Accordingly it has been found possible to continue these essential features to this day.

Again, the Exodus is closely associated with another religious rite, for Moses is said to have demanded liberty for the people to march three days' journey into the wilderness that they might sacrifice to their God.[1] This sacrifice is often identified with Passover, but the two are entirely distinct. For the same sources which record the demand agree in stating that Passover was celebrated on Egyptian soil and on the night of the Exodus. The fact that Passover at first required neither sanctuary nor priesthood made

[1] Exod. viii. 27.

this possible. On the other hand, the sacrifice for the celebration of which Moses claimed liberty for the people to leave Egypt bears all the marks of having been a חג or festival. It involved a journey or pilgrimage to a sanctuary. It was accompanied by a public sacrifice, in which the pilgrims took part. Because it was so public, Moses urged that the Egyptians could not fail to be offended by its outrage to their religious scruples. Further, its due celebration demanded an altar with the appropriate victims. In all these respects this sacrifice differed essentially from Passover. For, although in later usage it was forbidden to celebrate that rite elsewhere than at the sanctuary, and although it was associated with the festival of unleavened bread which was a חג, the two were never confused. Thus the single day of the Passover celebration was always considered to be an additional day to unleavened bread, and throughout the entire Old Testament the technical term of חג is never applied to Passover. When, therefore, Israel claimed liberty to go on pilgrimage into the wilderness, they asked for a new thing. What they demanded was permission to revive another practice of their religion which could not, as they carefully explained, be celebrated on Egyptian soil.

It would be possible to cite other evidence. But what has been offered is enough to prove that, before the promulgation of the Mosaic reform at Horeb, Israel was possessed of a religion, in the sense of a cult-practice, of its own. It already observed at least two rituals, one of a family, the other of a communal character. The men who restored the temple claimed the authority of Moses for the highly developed ritual which they instituted there. But, while such a claim must be set aside, the fact of its having been made shows that Israel traced the origin of its distinctive religion, cult as well as torah, to the period which immediately followed the Exodus. And there is evidence that sacrifices of a formal and public character attended the conclusion of the covenant at Horeb,[1] as they attended every covenant in the early period. Of the two rites to which reference has been made Passover must be considered later at some length, but there is not the same need, as indeed there is not the same possibility, to discuss the nature of the festival, for very little is known about its character, and very little about its peculiar elements. One or two matters, however, deserve recognition in connection with it. Thus a festival which implied a pilgrimage

[1] Notably in Exod. xxiv.

implied also a sanctuary dedicated to the deity in whose honour the rites were performed, and an altar on which the sacrifices were offered. Further, when Moses claimed liberty to lead his people to this shrine, he gave as his reason for leaving Egypt the plea that the ritual they must perform there could not fail to be offensive to the Egyptians. The sanctuary was one sacred to the God of Israel and the rites conducted there were peculiar to His worship, from which the people were not at liberty to deviate.[1] Since, then, the festival was communal and was observed at a common altar, the sacrifices could not have been left to the caprice of an individual or improvised. They must have been under the control of a priesthood.

From all that is known of that older world, the idea of a ritual, especially of a communal ritual, which was other than carefully regulated, and which was therefore in the hands of men who knew the ancestral customs, was wholly

[1] At Exod. viii. 27 Moses is made to state that the people will sacrifice to the Lord their God, " as He shall command." The clause in inverted commas may be an addition by the later legislators, who put the entire sacrificial ritual under Mosaic authority, or it may be original and be intended to emphasise that there could be no compromise in order to meet the king's wishes. In either case the phrase is characteristic for the ideas of the early period. Each god must have his own form of worship.

alien. Again, the recent discoveries at Ras
Shamra have served to confirm this judgment,
since the tablets contain references to specific
forms of sacrifice, each of which had its own
name. Israel, therefore, did not need to wait
until it arrived in Palestine before it came into
contact with a cult which was allied to those
of the heathen : it brought a more or less
developed system with it. Also this system pre-
ceded Moses, so that it did not bear the stamp
of his later reform. It represented a conception
of the divine character and of the relation
between God and man which belonged to an
earlier period in Israel's religious history. It
was there before the great leader introduced his
reform, and therefore belonged to that earlier
stage in the people's life about which very little
is clearly known. What we do know is that it
did not yet possess the definitely ethical character which became from the time of Moses the
nerve of Hebrew religion. Wanting that, it
equally failed to present a sharp contrast in
character between the God of Israel and the gods
of heathenism. The God whom the people
worshipped through their sacrifices was much
nearer the earth and more closely allied to
the nature-deities. The ritual-practices through
which they expressed and maintained the relation

to their God were conceived along the same lines. Like every other great religious reform, that of Moses was essentially a palimpsest; it was not written on a blank sheet of paper, but was superinduced on an already existing faith which not merely involved, but was embodied in a series of cult-practices. In this and other respects the reform of Moses closely resembled that of Mohammed, which also overlaid itself on the primitive faith of Arabia.

But the reform of Moses did not directly concern itself with the cult-practice of the nation : it aimed at something much more fundamental. Whether we accept the decalogue (in a shorter and simpler form) as Mosaic in its origin, or see in the ten words a later formulation of the aims of the great reformer, we must recognise there the leading convictions which constituted the movement. These principles were two, which were intimately connected.

On the one hand, Yahweh was the God of Israel, and Israel was the people of Yahweh. This mutual relation between God and nation was one in which Israel had no direct share : it had been instituted by Yahweh when He chose Israel for Himself. The election of the people had been made known to them, not by the covenant into which He entered with them at

Horeb, but by His sovereign act in delivering them from Egypt. The covenant and the decalogue followed the deliverance, and were intended to make clear the purpose which their God had with them in His act of redemption. Henceforth Israel must acknowledge no other god than Him who had intervened to make it a nation. On the other hand, Yahweh now revealed His nature and His will to the people which He had chosen, and He revealed these through covenant and decalogue, in which Israel might recognise the difference between their God and every other. His act of deliverance had been no mere forth-putting of His power, by which He proved Himself mightier than the gods of Egypt. He had isolated the people from the rest of their world in order that they might learn His will with them and the relation with Him into which He had brought them. Fundamental to this relation was that their God cared more for men's conduct to one another than for anything else. Yahweh was different from all other gods, because He counted righteousness of supreme significance. The people's relation to Him could only be maintained by a life which embodied this character of their God. Their conduct and their worship must alike bear the stamp of embodying and maintaining their relation to One who was ethical and spiritual.

A movement of this character did not deal in any direct way with the cult of sacrifice and festival which the people were actually practising in honour of their God. Nor did it attempt to prescribe a series of religious observances by which the relation to such a God could be maintained. The Mosaic reform left these matters aside : for the time it was sufficient to drive home the two convictions on which Israel's peculiar religion was based, and which gave it its distinctive character. Yet it is clear that these principles, however definitely expressed, and however pregnant in their consequences, could not in themselves constitute the basis of an active religion, and could not suffice to hold together the loose federation of the clans. It is equally clear that, without some means of maintaining their relation to their God, the work of Moses would have been half-done. Everything depended on the men's conviction that their freedom from Egypt and their new bond of unity had been due to the direct act of God who had intervened for their deliverance. But men cannot live upon a memory, even on the memory of an act of God. Unless their relation to the God of their deliverance

could be maintained by acts of faith, such as
make up an acting religion, each successive
generation would see the memory grow more
dim. The covenant at Horeb : Yahweh the
God of Israel, and Israel the people of Yahweh,
formed the rallying-cry for the nation, as the
simple creed of the Koran—no god but Allah,
and Mohammed His prophet—formed the battle-
cry of the Mohammedan. The early Moham-
medans framed an acting religion which, with
its practice of prayer, its Mecca pilgrimage,
and its observance of Ramadan, was the direct
outcome of their new faith. But they also, as
the customs at Mecca prove, continued rituals
which belonged to the past and which bore the
marks of a more primitive faith. It is impossible
to say whether Moses introduced any novel
practices into the religion of his people, for the
account we possess of his conduct is hopelessly
overlaid with material which makes him responsible for the developed cult of a much
later age. But it is significant to find Jeremiah
declaring in one of his oracles that Moses gave
no command about sacrifice or, indeed, about the
outward forms of his people's worship.[1] This
did not imply that the religion which Moses
founded and which Jeremiah believed himself

[1] Jer. vii. 21, 22.

to represent was hostile to, or even incompatible with, all outward acts of worship. It would be peculiarly inept to father such a position on Jeremiah, since he urged upon the exiles in Babylonia the practice of prayer, which is definitely a cult-act. The prophet was speaking to, and dealing with, a peculiar situation. Because his people were laying too great emphasis on the actual cult of their own time and were drawing the conclusion that God must preserve the temple where alone that cult could be duly performed, he must insist on the relative worth of the two factors of their ancestral faith. The ethical and spiritual elements of that faith were absolute and immutable, but the outward forms of worship were capable of being adapted in order to meet the needs of a changed time. He expressed this by the statement that the revelation at Horeb had said nothing about sacrifices and offerings. The significant feature there for the present subject is that a prophet could say quite naturally that Moses, when he founded Israel's religion, had not prescribed a cult.

To realise the situation of Israel at the time of the Mosaic reform, it is helpful to compare and contrast the position of the Church at its beginning. Like its forerunner, that represented a revival movement, which held a new conception of the divine nature, and therefore of the relation between God and man. It also was superinduced upon an older faith which had embodied itself in the sacrificial system of the temple and in the worship of the synagogue. One cannot fail to recognise how much it meant for the future of the infant Church that it was compelled to frame its own forms of worship. Its two sacraments, whether they were actually prescribed by Christ or developed later, were the direct outcome of the movement which they served to maintain and to propagate. Hence they were distinctive of the new faith and expressive of its genius. Wherever men came to use the ritual of the bread and wine, they did this because they were Christians. Wherever child or adult was baptised into the Name, they were baptised into the name of the Father and of the Son and of the Holy Spirit. In each case the rite which the Church observed was not merely an act of faith, it was an act expressive of its peculiar faith. The thoughts of those who practised these rituals of the cult and of those who witnessed them were carried back to the distinctive principles of the faith. The cult-acts had no meaning apart from this. In the same way, when the Church instituted its festivals,

D

each of these was directly associated with some event in the life of its Founder: every act of worship must carry men back to Him, in whose life and teaching it was founded.

It has at times occurred to me how different and how much more difficult the situation might have been, if the temple and the sacrificial system had not been swept away in the catastrophe of 70. Since all the apostles had been reared in the Jewish habits of worship, since after the Resurrection they continued to go up to the temple and to observe its forms, since the Lord Himself before His Passion went up to Jerusalem at the season of Passover, the young Church might have continued in its ritual practices some at least of the outward forms which belonged to Judaism. There might have appeared a new community, which believed in the Christ of the Gospels, but which followed a cult that had been framed to embody the convictions of the unreformed faith. When St Paul refused to bind his converts even to what remained of the old, the rite of circumcision, he was claiming that Christian men, in the acts which maintained their relation to God, must follow forms which were distinctively Christian.

The Mosaic reform, on the other hand, did

not make the same complete break with the past which was possible for the Church. The Mosaism to which the people committed themselves, when they entered into the covenant and into a federation based on that, and the cult which they had practised during their previous existence as separate clans did not spring from the same movement, and therefore did not represent the same convictions about the divine nature or about the nation's relation to its God. There was an antinomy, deep-seated and far-reaching, in Judaism from the period of its origin.

I have pointed out in another connection[1] that chapter v. of Deuteronomy shows some of the religious leaders of the nation to have been conscious of the distinction between the fundamental convictions which constituted the essence of the revelation through Moses and the actual religion which Israel practised in Palestine. They dated the ten words from the stay at Horeb and declared that they had been revealed directly, not to Moses alone, but to the whole nation. They also represented these ten words as having been inscribed on stone tablets, and brought them into no relation to the land to which the men were

---

[1] *Deuteronomy : the Framework to the Code*, chap. ii.

going. In this way the men declared that the
convictions as to the divine nature which were
embodied in the decalogue were immutable
and irrespective of place or time : they formed
the peculiar element which made the faith of
Israel different from that of the other nations.
On the other hand, the law which consisted of
judgments and statutes, *i.e.* the law which
governed the practical life and worship of the
nation, was not delivered at Horeb, but was
issued immediately before the entrance of the
people into Palestine. It was thus recognised
to have a different place in the national life from
the ten words : it was not immutable like the
laws chiselled in stone, and, unlike the decalogue, which belonged to every condition, it
was framed to meet the conditions of their
new life in Canaan. Yet the framing of this law
was committed to Moses at Horeb, and it was
promulgated with his authority on the other
side of Jordan. When the religious leaders of
the people thus referred the law which governed
their ordinary life and determined their religious
practices to the authority of Moses, they were
insisting that the civil law of Israel and its cult
must be in fundamental agreement with the
principles which their founder had taught. The
cult ought to embody and to maintain the con-

victions as to the nature of God and as to
Israel's relation to Him which were in the
ten words. For both derived from the same
source.

When the account in Deuteronomy dates this
law immediately before the entrance into Canaan,
and refers it to Moses, it is impossible to accept
its representation of history. Apart from every
other consideration, it conceives of the nation
as having practised no cult until it had arrived
at the borders of its new land. It thus contra-
dicts the early statement according to which
Moses claimed liberty for Israel in order that it
might practise its worship at a desert sanctuary.
But it is equally incompatible with the later view
which made Moses the author of the tabernacle
with its elaborate system of worship, which was
practised during the wilderness journey. The attitude which Deuteronomy takes to the people's
worship before the entry into Canaan stands
by itself, and on that account alone is very
remarkable. For, instead of regarding the entry
into Palestine as having coincided with a retro-
grade movement in the national religious practice,
it sets the worship after the conquest higher than
that which prevailed in the wilderness. The only
adequate explanation for such a position is that
the men were so dissatisfied with the character

of the worship which prevailed in the desert
that they deliberately refused to make the
founder of their religion responsible for it.
They reserved his authority for the cult which
arose on the soil of Palestine.   A somewhat
similar judgment on the worship of Israel,
while it was in the desert, appears in two of the
later prophets.   Thus in the book of Ezekiel [1]
it is said : " Moreover also I gave them statutes
that were not good, and judgments wherein
they should not live ; and I polluted them in
their own gifts, in that they caused to pass through
the fire all that openeth the womb, that I might
make them desolate, to the end that they might
know that I am the Lord."   The author of that
remarkable utterance agreed with the compilers
of the Deuteronomic code in the verdict they
passed on Israel's worship during the wilderness
period.   In that stage of their history the people
practised rites and offered sacrifices which were
not consonant with the character of Him in
whose honour they were performed.   On that
legislators and prophet are in agreement :
where they differ is in their conclusions.   The
legislators offered no explanation of the reason
why the past had been so unworthy : they were
content to say that a better condition came

[1] xx. 25, 26.

after the conquest, and that this was due to the influence of the Mosaic teaching. The exilic prophet could not stop there, because he was embarrassed by the theory that Moses instituted at Horeb the cult of the nation. The explanation he offered was another evidence of the straits into which theologians fall, when they argue from preconceived ideas. Again, Amos [1] reminded his hearers that during the forty years in the wilderness their fathers had brought sacrifices and offerings to gods whom they made for themselves.[2] During that period their worship had been of a character which Yahweh could not accept. In the pre-exilic period and even in the exilic period there were men who recognised the initial antinomy in their national religion. Israel's original worship had not been worthy of Him to whom it was offered.

The danger to Israel's religion after the settlement in Palestine was more profound and more many-sided than the mere attraction of the Canaanite worship. It arose from more than one cause. The sporadic character of the conquest contributed one element. Since the clans

[1] v. 25, 26.
[2] I quote only the clauses in the verses which are textually sound.

carried out their conquest in independence of one another and were for some time engrossed in the task of making good their new possessions, the federation sank into the background. As Yahweh was the God of the federation, this meant that their unity in a common faith grew more dim. It had not disappeared, since it could answer to a summons evoked by a common danger. That is what makes the incident of Barak's campaign so significant among the stories which have survived from the period of the settlement. The other tales recount the exploits of local leaders who championed the interests of their own clans, and who flung back invaders from the outside. Instead of these men receiving help from the other clans, they were occasionally hindered in their task by those from whom they might have expected help. When Samson was driven out of Dan, the men of Judah were prepared to assure their own security by handing him over to the Philistines. Gideon was hampered in his attack on the Midianites by the jealousy of his own tribesmen. But, when the danger threatened more than one tribe, there was a more general response to a challenge directed against Israel. Both accounts of the campaign emphasize therefore its religious character. In the poem the condition of Israel

seemed hopeless, until Deborah arose, a mother
in Israel.   In the prose account Barak refused
to move without the support of the prophetess.
The sense of the common danger awoke the
sense of racial unity, and with it the recognition
of the common faith.   Now that campaign was
waged against no invader from the outside, but
against the Canaanites.   Israel was conscious of
its distinction in race and in religion from its
Canaanite neighbours : but it needed some
special danger to evoke it, and the response was
not universal.

Another factor helped to weaken the distinctive character of the people's religion.   After
the settlement Israel accepted into the federation
the kindred clans which had never been in
Egypt.   These men had not learned, except at
second-hand, the reform movement under Moses.
Their religious practices bore the character of
their Semitic environment, and had therefore
been more liable to be tainted by those of the
Canaanites among whom they had been living.
Their accession to Israel brought an increase in
numbers, but a weakening in morale and in
religion.

Finally, there was the fatal resemblance between the cult of the new-comers and that of
their neighbours, whether these were Canaanites,

Moabites, or Ammonites. There was no great difference in the rituals which Israel practised, except that these were performed in honour of its own God. But, since this God required and received from His worshippers the same kind of offerings which other men brought in honour of Baal, He seemed to be the same in character as His rival. The distinction between Yahweh and Baal threatened to sink into nothing more than a difference in name. The danger did not come from outside, but from within the nation's life. Israel had not yet evolved a characteristic form of worship which would of itself turn the thoughts of those who took part in it to the peculiar character of its God. Besides, the Mosaic reform had now to be taken over by the second generation : and the history of every religion, as well as the experience of every missionary, is the sufficient proof that the testing time for the continuance of a movement arrives in the second generation.

To avoid this peril, which would have implied the disappearance of everything distinctive in the national life, it was essential to insist that Israel must reserve its allegiance to its own God. That is the burden of the Book of Judges with its record of the settlement in Canaan. The frame in which the series of stories has been set

reveals at once the purpose of the author or
editor.   According to him, the history of Israel
at that time illustrated one simple theme and
enforced one simple principle.   Ever and again
the people forgot Yahweh to follow the baalim
and ashtaroth, with the result that the Lord
delivered them into the power of their enemies.
When they repented and cried to the God of
their fathers, He raised up for them a deliverer.
But the writer was not theologising, nor was
he mastered by an abstract principle as to retri-
bution, or as to assured success being the reward
of such as served God loyally.   He was in his
own fashion insisting on a plain fact of history.
We should state it in different fashion and say in
much vaguer terms that whenever the nation
lost its sense of its distinctive character and of
the unity which sprang from that, it lost its
power of resistance.   The one thing on which it
could rally, and through which it could remain
strong to resist the influences to which it was
exposed, was its peculiar faith.

To illustrate his theme, the author has collected a number of tales which were current
in different parts of the country, from Dan
and Benjamin, from Ephraim and East Jordan.
These told the heroic deeds of the men who had
championed the cause of their people against

various invaders. Most of these are virile and so redolent of the soil that every reader can readily appreciate why they were treasured in the memory of the common people. Yet they do not convey quite so readily to a modern mind the impression that the men were precisely champions of religion. The accounts of two among them, where the hand of the editor is most manifest, may show his attitude and his method of dealing with his material in order to make it illustrate his point of view. In the original lusty saga of his prowess Samson appears as a stout man of his hands who was of course equal to any number of Philistines, and who displayed the somewhat crude humour that appeals to the peasant. What his fellow-countrymen remembered most was that he was from first to last devoted to Israel and that he died in its defence. It was the editor who made him a Nazarite, one who even before his birth was dedicated to Yahweh. From that sprang his devotion to the cause of his people. Again, it has long been recognised that behind the story of Gideon rests a simpler narrative which derived the defeat of the Midianites from a blood-feud that took its origin in the murder of the hero's brother by those marauders. The first success against the band led to Gideon having succeeded in expelling the Eastern invaders. It is again to the editor that we owe the record of the angel's visit to the hidden threshing floor and the account of how he marshalled his band for the night attack on the hostile camp. The inspiration of his resistance and the source of his victory are accounted for by his allegiance to Yahweh. Without its faith Israel, according to the historian, had nothing to fight for and no power of resistance.

The demand that Israel must reserve its allegiance to its own God was based on the conviction that He could tolerate no other god beside Him : the Lord your God is a jealous God. To recognise that this conviction emerged at this early date and that it remained to the end is to realise that it is of the very essence of Old Testament religion. In it was summed up the conviction that the God of Israel was different in character from all the other gods. No nature-religion can conceive of a deity which is jealous, except for reasons which admit of arrangement. One god might be jealous because he was not assigned so large a sphere of influence as another, or because he did not receive so large a share of offerings as seemed his due. But all that was needed in such a case was to refer the matter to the priests, who

delimited the spheres of influence or determined
the amount of offerings each received. After
that the gods took their place in a pantheon and
were content. But Yahweh did not come into
the category of the nature-gods. He had a
character which was His own and which He had
revealed to Israel. He had, therefore, something about which He could be jealous, about
which He must be jealous. If Israel gave its
allegiance to another god, it simply failed to
recognise the nature of Him who had made
Himself known to Moses. As Hosea said later,
it did not know Yahweh, if it could ascribe any
part of its national well-being to another than to
Him. By His very nature He must have all,
or He had nothing. If this feature in the character of their God had not been insisted on
after the settlement, when Israel took its place
in the world, if the leaders of the young nation
had not driven home that it must acknowledge
no other god, the work of Moses would have
broken down into heaps of sludge.

This conviction that Yahweh, because of His
unique nature, claimed the entire allegiance of
His people brought with it a conclusion which
bore directly on the national cult. The God of
Israel must have His own altars, His own forms
of worship, and His own priesthood. For the

people to worship at a heathen shrine or to adopt pagan rituals was to fail to realise the unique character of their own God. This is the burden of the Book of Deuteronomy and of the legislation in the early chapters of Leviticus. The codes are not exactly parallel. The code of Deuteronomy enters largely into the question of the heathen emblems and practices which were forbidden to Israel : that of Leviticus rather details the rituals which were peculiar to the holy nation. But both reveal the same aim : Israel's cult must be wholly its own. It is necessary to add that the view here taken of the purpose of the Deuteronomic Code does not rest on my individual judgment as to the extent to which this corpus of legislation was submitted to revision in the interests of centralisation of worship at Jerusalem. Even those who believe this revision to have extended over the whole law acknowledge the existence of an earlier law which demanded such revision. The original code before its revision was intended to serve a different purpose from that of centralisation. To use a convenient German phrase, it was drawn up to enforce *kultus reinheit*, not *kultus einheit*. Its purpose was to maintain the purity of Israel's forms of worship, and in that interest it commanded the nation to resort

only to its own altars and to maintain there its
own priests. It expressly forbade the use of
Canaanite symbols at these sanctuaries and the
practice of certain pagan rituals. The people
must break down the native altars, must abolish
the מצבות or standing-stones and must burn the
אשרות or sacred poles. Every emblem which
carried with it an association with Baal, and so
tended to confuse the essential difference between
Yahweh and the nature-gods must disappear
from Canaan. No symbol may remain beside
an Israelite altar which has an association with
heathenism, and so may turn the thoughts of a
worshipper away from his own God. In the
same way, certain practices were proscribed in
the name of religion : women and men were
forbidden to interchange clothes,[1] and it was
declared unlawful to make cuttings in the flesh
or baldness on the forehead in connection with
mourning for the dead.[2] The reason given for
these enactments is, in the one case, that Israel
was קדוש or set apart to the service of Yahweh,
in the other, that any one who conforms to the
practice is hateful to Yahweh. The fact that
the motives for condemning these and similar
customs were derived from the national religion
shows the purpose of the legislators. The acts

[1] Deut. xxii. 5.   [2] Deut. xiv. 1.

proscribed were rituals in the nature worship of Syria, so that any Israelite who adopted them acknowledged another god besides Yahweh. The recent discoveries at Ras Shamra have confirmed this conclusion, since they show that the practice of seething a kid in its mother's milk, a proscription which has long puzzled students of the Old Testament, was an ancient cult-practice. In these cases the legislators were insisting on the fundamental tenet of the Mosaic covenant, according to which Yahweh was the God of Israel. To worship Him with the emblems or by the rituals of paganism was to confuse the radical difference between the God of Israel and all other gods.

It was easy to draft and issue laws of this character. It must even have been comparatively easy to enforce them. Their purpose could be readily grasped by every Israelite, and it appealed to the people's growing sense of nationality. Above all, they did not interfere with the cult which the men were actually practising in honour of their God, and involved no change in their ancestral customs. At the utmost they may have interfered with the habits of the clans which had never been in Egypt and which, during their stay in Canaan, may have adopted the use of the standing-stones and

E

some of the forbidden rituals. Also, all the
religious leaders of the nation could heartily co-
operate in issuing and enforcing these regulations, though their motives in supporting them
may not have been identical. Such legislation
would appeal to the prophets who, according
to Amos [1] and Deuteronomy,[2] were the direct
outcome of the Mosaic reform, because the laws
in question maintained the unique character of
the God of Israel. It would equally appeal to
the priests, since the laws did not interfere with,
but rather strengthened, the people's loyalty to
their own forms of worship. Accordingly the
literature of the period before the rise of the
kingdom reveals no tension between these two
classes of religious leaders. Samuel acted as a
priest in Shiloh, where there already existed a
משפט, an altar-ritual which was so well known to
the people that they resented any change in it.[3]
Yet at Shiloh he received the revelation which
made him a prophet. As for Deuteronomy,
the characteristic feature of that code has long
been recognised to be the extent to which it
shows the influence of the prophetic school.

The case, however, was different as soon as
devout men began to turn their attention to
their ancestral cult and to ask whether all the

---

[1] ii. 11.   [2] xviii. 15, 16.   [3] 1 Sam. ii. 13.

forms of worship it prescribed adequately expressed their thought of the divine nature. The first task had been to insist that the God of Israel was different from the other gods, that He demanded the entire allegiance of His nation, and that He must be served at His own altars and after His own ritual. The second and more difficult task was to make clear wherein this difference lay and to make the difference patent in Israel's worship of Him. What made Yahweh distinct in His nature from all the other gods? The religious leaders of Israel could not escape from the question, and in particular the prophets who represented the Mosaic tradition were concerned with it from the time of Elijah to that of Jeremiah. Each of them appeared with a revelation which he claimed to have received directly from Yahweh, who had revealed Himself to him and through this had given him a commission to speak in His name. But none of them ever claimed to appear with a message which was wholly novel to his nation. What he had it in charge to declare was in the name of the God whom they all acknowledged, because He had made Israel the sphere of His self-revelation and had already made Himself known there. The self-revelation of Yahweh had been continuous in Israel, for He had

promised to raise up after Moses a prophet like
unto him.   Each new revelation must therefore
be in agreement with the initial revelation to
Moses; and the truth of any prophet's message
must be tested by whether it contradicted or
continued this.[1] There was common ground
which prophet and people occupied. Only the
prophet carried further what was involved in
the nature and will of God, and especially
developed its implications in relation to the
actual life of the nation. Every feature of that
life must correspond with the express will of
Him who had called it into being to know and
do His sovereign bidding.   Therefore the message of each prophet had two foci: it dealt with
the mind of Yahweh and with the actual life of
Israel as a more or less worthy response to that
mind. The institutions of the people must
serve that end.   The kingdom had more to fulfil in Israel than merely to protect its frontiers
or to unite its jealous tribes. As it was an
expression of the divine will, it must be unlike
the kingdoms of the other nations,[2] as unlike
those as Israel's God was unlike all other gods.
Israel's law courts must serve the same ends.
Through them every Israelite, whatever his
standing among his fellows, must be assured

[1] Deut. xiii. 1-5.   [2] 1 Sam. xii. 1-15.

that he will receive justice. Even justice was not sufficient. There must be no helpless poor in Israel, since the people were brethren, who together served a common God.[1]

But the judgment of the prophets, based as it was on the revealed will of God, could not stop short with the civil institutions of the nation. It must extend itself to the cult, the institution by which men sought to maintain their relation to their God. The acts by which men entered into relation to God, maintained it for themselves and their children, restored it when it was interrupted, must, more than any other part of their life, reflect the peculiar character of that relation, peculiar because their God was unique. At once there began to reveal itself the antinomy which had existed from the beginning between the revelation of the divine nature at Horeb and the actual cult by which Israel offered its worship. They were not based on the same principles.

Here it may be wholesome to realise a characteristic note in Old Testament religion. It was quite destitute of what is generally understood by a theology.[2] The Jew did not even

[1] Deut. xv. 4, 7–11.
[2] That may explain why we have no satisfactory book on Old Testament Theology, though several have attempted the task.

develop the abstract terms which are needed to formulate a system of thought. He thought seriously and reverently of the nature of his God, but he always conceived of the divine nature in terms of the divine purpose, as something which was not concerned with the world of ideas, but which passed over at once into the world of action. Right thoughts about God and His nature never seemed valuable in themselves, and they could not remain static in a system. The Jew has never formulated a creed, and especially he has never conceived that the acceptance of a creed qualified a man to be a member of the chosen race. Religion to him remained a way of life. For him right thoughts about God issued in conduct, in the things men did in their law courts, their fields, and their homes. To cheat one's neighbour, to seduce his bride, to commit perjury in the law courts was תועבה, an abomination to God. But right thoughts about God must, above all, translate themselves into the things men did at their sanctuaries in reverence to Him and with the purpose of maintaining their relation to Him. As soon as men began to think more seriously as to what constituted the distinctive character of their God, and therefore as to the peculiar relation in which they stood to Him, they could not fail to recognise with a growing sense of uneasiness that many of the things the people were doing at His altars accorded ill with His revealed nature. These rituals were fulfilled with the purpose of doing Him honour, but they were not turning the minds of the worshippers to their own God. As soon as this situation began to press on the minds of devout men in old Israel, there arose within the nation a tension, which was the outcome of a real difference of attitude. The religious leaders of Israel who had been at one, so long as their common aim had been to keep their people wholly devoted to their own God, began to take divergent ways. On the one side were the prophets with their sense of the purpose God had with the nation. As their knowledge of the scope and the character of this purpose deepened and clarified, the men began to realise that the native cult, even after it had been purified from pagan emblems, was not adequately fulfilling its end. Israel's working religion, its acts of faith, were being done in honour of Yahweh, but they were failing to supply to the worshippers true thoughts of Him. Men who have reached such a conviction will always speak strongly about a system which they believe to be an imperfect medium for the intercourse between a people and their God. But the effect of their criticism will often be to act as a leaven in slower minds and to lead gradually to a recasting of the system. In my judgment such a situation can be paralleled in every higher form of religion, and, when the movement for reform is wisely directed on both sides, it can result in preventing a danger which besets every cult—the danger of falling into a series of meaningless forms. It was bound to appear more intensely in early Judaism because of the initial antinomy within that faith.

But the opposition between priest and prophet during the period of the monarchy was neither so extreme nor so violent as it has often been represented. So far as the prophets were concerned, I have already pointed out that convictions which they held necessarily involved some means for maintaining the relation between the people and their God. As far as the priests were concerned, it is an equal exaggeration to suppose them to have been utterly deaf to the prophetic message so that they refused to learn anything from it. One simple fact is enough to warn us from adopting this easy solution of the relations between the two bodies of religious teachers. We to-day should never have known anything of the messages of the prophets but for the pious care with which their oracles were collected, edited, and included in the sacred writings during the period of the Exile and that of the Return. Yet the men who fulfilled this task and who commended these books to the faithful must have been closely associated with the community which built the second temple and with the priests who conducted the sacrificial worship there. These men would never have reverently preserved the trenchant criticism which had been levelled against the cult unless they had believed it to be compatible with the continuance of a cult. The same men who restored the sacrificial system and who made the temple the centre of the new Jewish polity were also careful to collect these oracles. But men preserve for the guidance of the future and commend to the attention of their followers that from which they themselves have profited.

Men who are convinced of the mischievous character of some system which they find in control of the life of their fellow-men will always express those convictions strongly. And they will often speak with more vehemence when they discover that their intention has been misunderstood and even misrepresented by slower and more conservative minds. The prophets found arrayed against them the tenacity with which men cling, especially in everything which touches their religious customs, to old and familiar forms which have grown to be part of their very life. Naturally this opposition appeared most strongly among the priests, whose function it was to conduct these forms, and who were inclined to call a halt as soon as the ancestral rituals had been protected from the taint of the foreign religion. But, from what we know of men's habits in religion, it would be an equal mistake to conclude that the priests were alone in their opposition, or that they were governed by the baser consideration that by this craft they had their living. Every minister of religion who has or has had the privilege and the responsibility of guiding the worship of a community knows how hard it is to effect even a minor change in matters of ritual. Within the Evangelical Church, where the sacraments are simpler in their form of celebration and where the worshippers are less bound by tradition, opposition will rise over any movement which touches the dear familiar customs which have woven themselves into the life of a generation.

That was the source of the undoubted tension

which arose under the kingdom between some of the prophets and the priesthood in old Israel.[1]

[1] I have written " some of the prophets," because we have no right to conclude from the fact that all the prophets whose oracles have reached us took a critical attitude towards the cult, that there were no prophets who took a different attitude. Certainly in relation to other questions which then emerged, there was no such unanimity in the prophetic school. When Micaiah ben Imlah uttered his verdict on Ahab's policy he was in a hopeless minority among his brethren at the king's court; and Jeremiah was in like case when he gave his opinions on the political situation in the audience chamber of Zedekiah. Prophets were no more unanimous in old Israel than they have shown themselves since.

There is also evidence that a prophet was employed in connection with the cult at the celebration of the Feast of Tabernacles, see p. 130 infra. Probably the recognition of these facts has led some students of the Old Testament to begin to use the expression " cult-prophets."

III

ITS CHANGE THROUGH THE INFLUENCE OF THE PROPHETS

IN the closing paragraphs of the last chapter the suggestion has been made that the undoubted tension between prophet and priest which appears during the period of the kingdom was not due to a radical divergence in principle. The two bodies of men who had in charge the guidance of the religious life of their nation held much in common. They were equally convinced of the necessity to keep Israel loyal to the God who had revealed His nature and His will to His people. They were also convinced of the need for some forms of worship which both expressed and maintained the relation between the nation and this God. They *may*, further, have realised that the cult, as it was actually celebrated, was not fulfilling its work, and that some change was needed to adapt it to its purpose. But the part which prophet and priest had to fulfil in connection with this change was very different. The prophet must enunciate, as clearly as he might, the great convictions which were essential to the religion of Israel. He must also have the courage and the insight to declare that the rituals among which he himself had been reared were in many respects in hopeless contradiction to the character of Him in whose honour they were celebrated. The priest's part in the matter was more practical and humdrum. He could not fail to realise how deeply the cult had twined itself into the life of the nation, and that it is always easier to change the thoughts of men than their habits. He must be patient with the slow-moving minds of peasants, and dare not, by too large and sudden changes, lose the confidence of men whom he must seek to lead into new ways. The difference between priest and prophet was one of tempo rather than of principle.

These suggestions, however, are obviously too general in their character to be accepted without proof. It remains to ask whether any evidence can be brought to support such a view of the relation between the two bodies of religious leaders. Was the Hebrew cult during the earlier period an immutable thing, or can we discover evidence of its having undergone change? If it was modified in any direction, what was the character of the change which passed over it? In particular, is it possible to trace a connection between this change and the attitude of the prophetic school? If that should be possible, it will prove that the prophets were not ineffectual

in which it is possible to cite a proof for the continuance of the custom, is connected with the southern kingdom. On the other hand, the story of Abraham and Isaac, which forbade it, is generally assigned to the account of the origins of Israel which comes from Northern Israel. This points to the rite having been first forbidden in the northern kingdom, where the prophetic movement made its earliest appearance and reached its strongest influence. When this is combined with the other fact that it was condemned in Judah by another prophet, it becomes clear that the rejection of human sacrifice derived from the prophetic school of thought. The men pronounced such a sacrifice illegitimate because it conflicted with their convictions as to the character of Yahweh. They were judging their own cult in the light of conceptions of what their God required, which came to them from the Mosaic revelation.

That human sacrifice was set aside on the ground that it conflicted with the character of the God of Israel appears from the terms in which the offering of Isaac was forbidden. In other cases where mention is made of the rite, men turned to it because they were in some grave danger. Either the nation was in extreme peril or the individual was in sore straits of conscience.

No such peculiar conditions attended Abraham at the time when he resolved to offer his first-born. As an individual the man was in no need of atonement for himself or his household, and there is no hint in the narrative of such a purpose or such an effect having been connected with his offering. Also, instead of the sacrifice having availed for the deliverance of the nation, it seemed rather to endanger all its future, since Isaac was the boy in whom every hope for the future of Israel centred. Further, it is deliberately stated that the patriarch's readiness to offer up his only son might be construed as due to a desire to honour God. That is the sense which attaches to the statement that Elohim put it into Abraham's mind to offer up his son, while Yahweh forbade it. The use of the two divine names has led many commentators to follow the usual course of recognising here a double document, and on that basis to divide the narrative into two. But the story defies the easy solution of the use of the scissors.[1] What the writer wished to say was that the motive which led the patriarch to his decision was or could be construed as a divine prompting. It was not due to any selfish fears on Abraham's part, or prompted by anxiety

[1] Skinner acknowledged the fact in his volume on Genesis I.C.C. *ad loc.*

F

for his personal safety.   He desired by his deed
to honour his God and to bring a supreme proof
of his devotion.   The father of the faithful, who
represented Israel, was as ready as any heathen
devotee to prove the entirety of his self-sacrifice
to his God.   The lovely and moving scene
between father and son was not written from
artistic motives, but was intended to convey a
religious message.   The writer made Abraham
carry out his resolve almost to the end—he had
already lifted up the knife to slay his son.   Only
in the supreme moment was his purpose arrested,
and it was arrested by a messenger of Yahweh.
Even when such a sacrifice was prompted by
the highest motives, it was forbidden in Israel.
The God of Israel willed no such offerings, and
absolutely rejected them through a message to
the first father of the race.   They were not consonant with the character which He had revealed
to the nation, or with the relation which He
had instituted between them and Himself.   The
revelation of the nature of its God, which was
peculiar to Israel, was having its inevitable effect
on the cult by which His people worshipped
Him.

Another cult-practice which was forbidden in
Israel was that of religious prostitution, whether
by men or women.   The terms in which the

prohibition was issued[1] show that the custom had once held a place in the Hebrew cult. For the legislators did not forbid it in the language which they generally employed when they referred to the Canaanite rituals or emblems. In relation to such foreign practices they based their rejection as a rule on the ground that Israel was holy, in the sense of being set apart to Yahweh. They thus expressed their conviction that, as Yahweh claimed the undivided allegiance of His people, so He must be worshipped at His own altars and with His own emblems. On the other hand they declared everything connected with religious prostitution to be תועבה, or abomination to Yahweh. The practice was condemned, not because it was foreign, but because it was inconsistent with the character of their own God. The prohibition was directed against a rite which had once existed in Hebrew religion.

To understand the existence of such a custom it is useful to recognise the place of, even the justification for, religious prostitution in a primitive nature-religion. The chief function of every nature-god was to maintain the processes of nature, especially those which were directly helpful to man. The aim of the worship offered

[1] Deut. xxiii. 17–18.

to such a god was to ward off anything in these
nature processes which might prove hurtful to
the community, and to maintain everything
which was helpful to its continuance and well-
being. Naturally, in connection with the last
aim, the leading act on the part of the god was
to promote fertility, whether in the crops or
among the flocks and herds on which the life of
the people depended, or in the men and women
themselves, without which the life of the tribe
ceased. To declare a certain number of women
קדשות or holy, in the sense that they were set
apart to the service of the god, was to place the
eternal function of woman, her maintenance of
life, under the protection and furtherance of the
deity. Since these women represented the continuance of life in the tribe, their dedication to
the divine service implied that the fertility on
which the life of the people in the last issue
depended, was set under the charge of the tribal
god, and so was assured. When the custom
is correlated to the conception of the character
of the deity in a primitive nature religion, it
becomes possible to recognise that its original
purpose was reasonable and even deserved
respect.

As soon, however, as the character of the God
of Israel was conceived in the light of the

revelation at Horeb, the entire attitude to such a custom was changed. The nation had learned to believe that Yahweh had intervened to deliver it, and that it was His purpose to preserve those whom He had called His peculiar people. At once the custom of religious prostitution lost its *raison d'être*. It became what the legislators in Deuteronomy called it, תועבה, something which was grotesquely dissonant with the nature and will of the God who had revealed Himself to Israel. From the period of the Mosaic reform the practice was doomed. The issue of a law against it in the Deuteronomic code is the proof that the religious leaders of the nation had recognised the incongruity. But a torah, dealing with the cult-practice, must have had the imprimatur of the priests before it could be forbidden to bring the hire which resulted from the custom into the house of the Lord. On the other hand, the driving force behind the law came from the prophetic message as to the character of God. Priest and prophet were combining, not merely in safeguarding their people from corruption by a foreign cult, but in purging the cult of Israel from its baser elements.

The two illustrations which have been selected may be sufficient to show one method in which the religious leaders of the nation dealt with their cult. How far the same motive influenced the men in their rejection of certain Canaanite customs it it impossible to pronounce with any certainty. Yet it may have been present when they forbade, *e.g.*, men to wear women's garments and vice versa. That custom, like religious prostitution, was associated with Syrian nature worship, and, so far as is known, had never formed part of the native cult of Israel. It may have been forbidden to the tribes which came up from Egypt, because it implied a recognition of the Syrian goddess, and so conflicted with their absolute allegiance to Yahweh. But if the tribe of Asher had been settled in Canaan before the conquest, it may have adopted some of these rites to which its situation in the north peculiarly exposed it. In that case the law forbidding these must have interfered with the actual cult of the tribe, and the motive which led to the ban upon them may have been derived from their being תועבה, wholly incompatible with the revealed character of Yahweh. Here and elsewhere it is likely that the two motives combined to produce a common result.

The religious leaders of the nation were not, however, content to put under the ban certain features of their cult which were offensive to the revealed character of their God. They also

transformed a number of their native rituals,
and they did this in two ways. In connection
with some of these they retained, so far as we
know, the original form of the rite, and were
satisfied with supplying new motives which
changed its meaning. In other cases they went
further and altered the outward form as well as
the intention. It is necessary to examine their
procedure in both directions in order to determine, if possible, what influenced them in the
alterations they thus made.

The outstanding instance of the first-mentioned
method was Passover, which presents certain
advantages for the present inquiry. Thus it is
not necessary to bring proof of the native
character of the rite, since Passover is generally
acknowledged to have belonged to Israel before
its entry into Palestine. It is also sure that the
method of its observance was considerably
changed at different periods in the national
history. Yet the leading features of the pre-
Mosaic ritual have been preserved with sufficient
fulness to make it possible to recognise the
original form and even the original purpose
of the rite.

This early ritual appears in a double form in
Exodus xii. 1-14, 21-28, where the second of
the two passages is more important, since it

reveals more clearly the purpose it was originally
intended to serve. In it there is mention of a
משחית, or destroyer, who was believed to be
peculiarly active on that special night in the year.
Not only was he at large, but, as his name
proves, his presence boded mischief. How
mischievous his presence would be, if he could
once make his way into the homes of the people,
is shown by the character of the rite which was
performed then. A lamb was slaughtered, but
there was no altar and no priest, nor was any
use made of the sacred fat. The main purpose
in slaying the lamb was to secure the blood,
which was then daubed on the lintel and doorposts of the cottage in which the family had
assembled. Accordingly the blood was not
intended to serve the end of a sacrifice in honour
of " the destroyer " : its purpose was to act as
a prophylactic which kept the intruder at bay.
By its application to doorposts and lintel the
house was turned into a sanctuary for the time
being, into which the prowler of the midnight
dark could not enter. Therefore the people
were strictly warned that they must not venture
beyond the limits of the guarded house : to
do this was to expose themselves to the power
of the spirit on the night of its power. The
purpose of the ritual was not to honour, but to

ward off, the fatal power of this destroyer. Its dominating note was fear, not reverence.[1]

It is generally recognised that this crude ritual was modified under the influence of the Mosaic reform, but the natural effect of underrating the character of the reform itself has been to obscure the radical alteration which was made in Passover. Thus it is explained that, in consequence of the command laid on Israel to reserve all its allegiance to its own God, no acknowledgment of the power of the destroyer could be permitted. Passover must be celebrated with a reference to Yahweh alone. The change, it has further been suggested, was the more easily effected because Yahweh at this early stage of the national history was not fundamentally different from such a night-demon. Indeed, the fact that Yahweh was thus substituted for the destroyer is at times employed as the proof of the low development of religious thought even at the time of Moses. But this is to ignore the extent of the change which came over the whole rite. Thus, so far from Yahweh taking the

---

[1] The מַשְׁחִית of the Exodus presents an interesting resemblance to the spirit which attacked Jacob at the ford of Jabbok, and to the other which assailed Moses when he left Midian to return to Egypt. In those cases it is equally suggestive to notice how the later writers, to whom we owe the accounts, dealt with their original material.

place of the night-demon, it is expressly stated
that Yahweh shall deliver Israel from its fear
of the destroyer. This, it must be recognised,
does not deny the existence of the demon, it
does not even deny his power. What it does
deny is that he has any power over the nation
to deliver which Yahweh has intervened: he
may still have power over the nation which does
not acknowledge the protection of Israel's God.
Accordingly, the whole character of the night
has been changed. Instead of being the night
of the destroyer's power, it has become the night
of Yahweh's power: as such it is a night much
to be remembered of Israel, because then its God
came down to deliver His own. Where once
men cowered behind the protecting blood daubed
on doorposts and lintel lest the demon entered
to slay them, they now celebrated a rite which
recalled the hour when their God led them
into liberty and made them a nation. The
character of the rite was changed precisely
because the character of the deity who was
recognised in it had become different. Certain
obstinate features of the old ritual were continued with the tenacity which belongs to old
religious practice. In one case an attempt was
made to give one such feature an explanation in
at least apparent agreement with the new meaning

which attached to the whole. The daubing of doorpost and lintel with the protective blood had its significance so long as the destroyer was central in the thought of the people, but it was hopelessly incongruous with the thought of the advent of Him who came to redeem Israel from Egypt. So it was supplied with a lame interpretation that when Yahweh went abroad through the land of Egypt, He should by its presence be able to distinguish the homes of the Israelites. But its incongruity with the prevailing character of the rite was so obvious that this original feature disappeared. When Passover was celebrated at a sanctuary instead of in the home, the blood of the lamb was treated like that of any other sacrifice : it was dashed against the altar. No attempt, however, was ever made either to maintain or to rationalise the command that no one dare leave his sanctuary dwelling until the dawn had pronounced the end of the demon's night of power. By no ingenuity of interpretation could that be brought into harmony with the belief that on this night of nights in its history Israel had marched out into a liberty which it owed to the grace of its God.

It is possible to institute a comparison between the Jewish procedure in dealing with Passover and the method by which the Christian Church transformed the pagan festival of the winter solstice into its Christmas celebration. Like Judaism, Christendom made the day one to be ever remembered, the first festival in the Christian year. But it would be a meagre idea of the change which the Church wrought to say that it merely substituted the name of Jesus for that of the god in whose honour the original rite was observed. It would be a travesty of its act to conclude that the change was more easily effected because of the initial resemblance between the two deities. The new name carried with it a novel connotation, so that everything in the ritual took on new meaning. When the Christ-child in His cradle became the centre of adoration, the rite was transformed from within. What had been a nature-festival associated with the return of the sun, became a memorial of the Advent of Him who came to redeem. Instead of a form of nature religion came a worship which was historic and redemptive in its character. In the same way, though Passover retained much more of its primitive features, fundamentally its whole orientation was altered as soon as it was transferred to Yahweh. Now, instead of marking the night of power for the demon of the dark, it reminded Israel of how its God had intervened to redeem. As He delivered His people from bondage to Egypt, so He delivered it from fear of the destroyer. The note of the entire rite was changed: instead of fear came confidence and joy. The God of Israel was no nature power: He was the God who in one great historic act had come down to save.

Passover was a palimpsest, like the religion of which it formed a leading feature. In the background appeared the characteristics of a lower type of religion, which had undergone the transforming influence of a higher faith. The motives which effected this transformation were taken from the historic and redemptive character of Yahwism, and so were directly derived from the Mosaic reform. That reform prefaced even its law with a statement of the nature of Him in whose name it was issued: "I am the Lord thy God who brought thee out of the land of Egypt." As the law was countersigned with the nature of the Lawgiver, so the cult-act of the people must turn their minds to the recognition of what He had been and was to them. Priest and prophet combined in making a leading ritual in the cult express more adequately the character of their common God.

The change which was thus made in Passover,

as soon as it was celebrated in honour of Yahweh, illustrates one broad effect which came over the temper of the nation as the result of the command to reserve its entire allegiance to its own God. The primitive rite had not been performed in honour of the spirit, or even to propitiate it : its intention was to keep the destroyer at bay. This, of course, implied that his power was essentially malign : to know that he was loose in the midnight dark sent every weak thing cowering behind protection. The dominant note of such a religion was fear, and its ceremonial largely consisted in rites and spells which had power to protect the devotees against the unseen beings that filled earth and air. Early Israel shared this attitude to the world in which it lived with the other nations of the time. The men of that period felt themselves to be little and weak in face of a nature of which they were profoundly ignorant, and which they did not conceive to be governed by any law. The events which might sweep away a man or his property, an earthquake, or a blight, a swarm of locusts or a pestilence, were not natural phenomena to him : they were extraordinary or supernatural, and were the work of the evil spirits which were active in every department of nature and in every part of man's

life. Even so trivial a circumstance as tooth-
ache took its rise from such a source. Sir James
Frazer has written a passage of superb English
in which he has described the attitude of men
under those conditions, even in so advanced a
civilisation as that of Babylonia. Unfortunately it is too long to be quoted here, and to
attempt to convey its force by extracts would
only spoil the effect of its massive and cumulative
description. But in it he has brought out
how to the ordinary Babylonian the world was
peopled with spirits, from whose influence no
man might hope to escape, whether by day or
night, whether by land or sea, whether in the
sown land or on the open desert. He has also
pointed out the dreadful iteration with which
recurs the formula about them—they are evil,
they are evil. For all their influence was conceived to be malign, so that man's life was
dominated continually by fear. The best for
which any man dared hope was that by the
recital of the correct incantations or the performance of the right ritual he might keep these
dreaded powers at bay.

The paralysing power of such an attitude to
nature has largely disappeared out of modern
life through the increase of knowledge. Man-
kind has learned that nature is not governed

by mere caprice, but is itself subject to law. The laws which govern many of its operations have been discovered, so that man lives in comparative security because he knows how in many cases he can protect himself, and he also knows where he must submit. Even where the cause of any phenomenon has not been traced, man has been able to persuade himself that there is a cause. The result has been to deliver men from fear of the unknown, since at the worst nature is merely indifferent to much which men prize, and pursues her majestic course unmoved by pity or by anger. Early Israel could not find that way of escape; to it as to the rest of its world nature's operations were directly controlled by supernatural influences. But a way of escape from the fear of the unknown which could not come by science came through religion. Israel learned to believe that there was only one power which men needed to consider at all, for their world was controlled by one sovereign purpose to one end. Behind it was the will of Yahweh. All who devoted themselves to Him were delivered from every other fear : the fear of the Lord was a strong tower. The world was no longer controlled by caprice, so that at any moment the dreaded forces in it could work their malicious will on the people. It was not only in the hands of the One, but of One who had a mind toward His people which He had revealed to them. He had intervened for their deliverance, and by that act on His part had declared Himself to be Israel's God, and Israel to be His people. In the initial act of the Passover night He had made known what Israel could always expect at His hands, for then He made Himself known. The demand that Israel should reserve all its allegiance to Him was thus no new burden which He laid on the nation. It was the other side of the deliverance which He had wrought for them. In itself it was a deliverance from the fear which beset their lives, for it unified their world and gave them foothold and confidence through the sense that it was under the control of One who meant well by them.

Islam has owed much of its success, and still owes much of its growing power among the backward races of Africa, to the same cause. Its simple dogma of the unity of God, whose sovereign will governs the world, is able to do for these races something of what Yahwism brought to the early Hebrew. When one realises the condition of terror of the unknown which prevails in the African bush, and recognises how easily it can return as it has done in

Hayti, one realises more clearly the debt which humanity in its sore travail has owed to a faith which could deliver it from the nameless fear of the demons of the dark.

It would be possible to follow this line of study in connection with the bread of the presence.   There is a passage [1] which points to this offering having originally consisted of more than the shewbread. The table, which was reserved for the daily presentation of these cakes, and the other vessels, dishes, spoons, flagons, and bowls, which accompanied the cakes on this table, point to the whole having been once interpreted as food, literally intended for the consumption of the deity to whom it was presented. The cakes of bread formed the last remnants of a complete meal.   While, however, these remained they received a new interpretation. The idea of Yahweh, the giver of Palestine to His nation, and the One on whom it was dependent for its daily needs, being in any way Himself dependent on the gifts of the faithful, became intolerable in Israel ; and the constant presentation of the bread of the presence became an acknowledgment that the nation owed everything to His bounty. Two features of the later cult indicate that this was

[1] Exod. xxv. 23–30.

the motive which guided the change in the ritual. On the one hand, so early as the time of David, it was evidently the practice for the cakes to be eaten at the sanctuary, though precautions were taken to prevent them from coming into the hands of men who were not ceremonially clean.[1] In New Testament times it appears to have been the regular practice for the food to be consumed by the priests.[2] Now, while the priests consumed these offerings in other religions, where a banquet was set out for the god, the pretence was maintained that the food was actually consumed by the deity.[3] Where the old conception of the god as claiming or even needing food from his worshippers still prevailed, it was necessary to maintain the fiction that he had eaten it. Only because Israel had departed from the original idea of the purpose of the presence-bread, could it frankly give it a different destination. On the other side, in the old use of Jerusalem which forms the basis of the early chapters of Leviticus, the offerings of the faithful are called לחם, the food or bread of Yahweh. The Septuagint has substituted a more colourless word for the definite expression.[4]

---

[1] 1 Sam. xxi. 6. [2] St Matt. xii. 4.

[3] Witness the trick by which Daniel is said to have exposed the imposture among the Babylonians in *Bel and the Dragon*.

[4] *Cf.* e.g. Lev. iii. 11.

Evidently the translators felt the incongruity of the phrase with the fundamental attitude as to the purpose of the offerings in their own faith.

In the same way the remarkable ritual of the scapegoat appears to have been originally an annual rite which was peculiar to the neighbourhood of Jerusalem. Certain features in connection with it suggest that in the earlier period it was performed with no direct reference to Yahweh. The ideas which it embodies as to sin, and as to the means for its removal, show close affinities with ideas which prevail, not only among the Semitic nations, but in other quarters. But in some period before or after the Return the rite was transferred to Yahweh, and at once the grosser elements in it began to be purged away. The process was begun by which the Day of Atonement has been transformed into one of the most remarkable and spiritual factors in the religion of modern Israel.

When they are taken by themselves, these two ritual-practices do not justify the inference that they were transformed in Israel by the desire to make the native cult more worthy of the character of Him in whose honour they were carried out. There can be no question as to the fact of their having been radically modified, while the old form was retained. Nor

can there be any doubt that the modification
they received was all in the direction of a more
ethical and spiritual conception of God.   But
our information in regard to them both, and to
their history, is meagre, so that it is impossible
to say dogmatically that they formed part of
Israel's native cult.   Especially is this the case
in connection with the ritual of the scapegoat.
Any conclusions which can be formulated about
its locus and about its original purpose must
always be tentative.   They rest very largely
on resemblances between it and similar cult-
practices in other faiths, and for that reason are
peculiarly open to question.   For, although the
craft of discovering analogies and resemblances
between religions which are as different in their
character as they are distant in space is lustily
pursued, it ought never to be pursued as though
it constituted proof of identity of origin or of
intention.   Apart from any other consideration,
it is generally carried on with an entire neglect
of the far more numerous differences which exist
among the same faiths.   It remains possible,
however, that the rite of the scapegoat may have
passed into the cult of Israel after David's
conquest of Jerusalem and may have belonged
to the original Jebusite inhabitants of the city.
The probability of borrowing is not so high

in the case of the bread of the presence, since it was evidently well established before David's accession to the throne.

Both rites may have been adopted by Israel after its settlement in Palestine, and both may have been accepted by Judah during the period of its isolation from the rest of the tribes. It deserves attention that the presence-bread only appears in a sanctuary which was dependent on Jerusalem, and in connection with the tabernacle, which reproduces the usage of the second temple, and that, as has been stated, certain features in the rite of the scapegoat point to an original connection with the city. In the more conservative southern kingdom, which was less influenced by the prophetic movement, the priests did not denounce the usages as heathen, but as little did they retain them in their old form. For both of them appear in the Israelite cult with new motives and so greatly changed that we must read between the lines, as it were, in order to recognise their original significance. It is probable, but cannot be called certain, that the revealed character of the God of Israel was remoulding the worship by which the people maintained their relation to Him.

IV
CULT RUBRICS AND CONCLUSION

IT is possible to group together a number of other cult-practices in early Israel, and to recognise that they have been modified in order to make them more worthy means for conveying the specific content of the national religion, and for maintaining the peculiar relation between Israel and its God. These differ from the rites which have already been passed in review in two respects. The method which was followed in adapting them to their purpose was different. Also we are badly informed as to the early history of these usages. It is impossible to pronounce with confidence whether they all belonged to the primitive worship of the nation, or whether they may not, or some of them may not, have been borrowed after the conquest. It is equally impossible to decide what may have been their original form, and so to recognise any changes which may have been made in that outward form. What can be done in relation to them is to detect any feature in them which bears evidence of being derived from Israel's peculiar religion, to examine its character and so to conclude as to the reason which led to its introduction. That will be enough to prove that, whatever their source may have been, and whatever the purpose they originally served, they have been submitted to a process which brought before the Israelites who took part in them the distinctive characteristics of their own religion. They had always been acts of faith: they became acts of the peculiar faith of Israel.

Here it may be useful to consider the general question of the origin of one leading feature of the Israelite cult during the period of the kingdom, the three festivals of the sacred year. Evidently these bulked largely in the life of the nation, for they appear in all the codes, and hold a prominent place in the prophetic oracles. It is commonly and confidently stated that rites which are so closely related to agriculture and dated by its seasons must have been wholly alien to Israel during its nomadic life. Yet the proof rests ultimately on the judgment that the rite, for the due performance of which the people claimed to leave Egypt, was Passover. Since, in my judgment, the two were entirely distinct, I must conclude that the practice of pilgrimage to a sanctuary with the accompaniment of altar and sacrifice belonged to the clans in Egypt.

That does not necessarily imply a cycle of such festivals or their intimate association with agriculture, but it does imply the existence of a communal festival in which all the tribes united. Such a practice, which had been made the basis for the claim to leave Egypt, and which had received a new significance through the actual Exodus into liberty, was sure to be continued. Besides, its utility in their new condition and needs was too obvious and great for it to be permitted to lapse. It served the purpose of an embryo Amphictyonic Council for the clans. Not only did such a communal festival, at which all the males were required to appear, gather the scattered clans to a common centre and maintain their sense of unity, which was apt to disappear in the desert. It also brought into the foreground the one bond of their loose federation, their allegiance to Yahweh, the God of the federation. When they met at the bidding of their religion, their devotion to this religion was strengthened, and at the same time the sense of their unity and of their difference from the rest of their world was renewed. Accordingly it is natural to find that, as soon as the confusion which attended the conquest was past, and life in the new country took on greater order, the annual festival appeared. Elkanah was in

the habit of going up to Shiloh every year.[1]
While, however, it is legitimate to suppose that
the Israelites brought with them the custom of
an annual pilgrimage to a sanctuary and continued
it in their new country, it is not so clear that they
maintained there only their native rituals, and
did not develop these more largely by borrowing
features from the Canaanites or from the tribes
that had been longer settled in Palestine. The
transition from the desert life to the new conditions, where the men became fellahin, could
hardly have failed to effect a change in the character of the offerings. The people had refused
to celebrate their festival in Egypt because it
involved sacrifices which must prove obnoxious
to the Egyptians. This, combined with the fact
that in Goshen they had kept cattle, implies that
the chief element at least in the worship had
consisted of animal sacrifices. But now, when
the men had succeeded to the fields, olive yards,
and vineyards of Palestine, place must be found
for a new type of offerings. The novel forms
of sacrifice would naturally bring with them

[1] 1 Sam. i. 21. Unfortunately we do not know whether
the sanctuary there served merely the local tribe of Benjamin
or a larger constituency. From the fact, however, that there
was a היכל, a regular building at Shiloh, and from the other
fact that Samuel is called an Ephraimite, it is likely that the
festival there gathered more than the local farmers.

their appropriate ritual forms. Further, the men's new and intimate association with the farmer's year must have had an influence on their worship. They could enlarge the scope of their cult, so that it covered and influenced all the leading features of their new life. The festivals became more numerous,[1] and at the same time the cult in connection with them grew richer and more developed.

An evidence of the close connection between the sacred year and the natural year of Palestine appears in the dates of the three festivals, as these appear in the early calendar in Deuteronomy xvi. Unleavened Bread was to be celebrated at the time " when thou puttest thy sickle into thy standing corn," and so fell at the period of the barley harvest. Pentecost followed seven weeks later, and coincided with

[1] I have always thought that some such development is needed to explain why the Feast of Tabernacles retained to the end the significant title of החג, the festival *par excellence*. Not only were the sacrifices at this period more abundant, but Tabernacles was the only festival in the year at which every Israelite, man, woman, and child, even the stranger within the gates, was required to be present. If, now, Tabernacles had been from the beginning distinctively Israelite, and if it had come to be associated in the mind of the nation with its deliverance from Egypt, the prominence given to it would find a natural explanation. Passover and Tabernacles, a spring and an autumn rite, a family and a communal observance, would then be native to Israel.

the time of the wheat harvest. When, with the ripening of the grapes, olives, and figs the harvest was complete, Tabernacles closed the cycle. There was an obvious advantage in this : a people's methods of worship should be sufficiently flexible to be capable of being brought into contact with their daily life. Without some such adjustment the outward forms of their cult might have become an interesting, but pointless, anachronism. But there was an equally obvious danger, since forms of worship which were closely influenced by the life of nature could not fail to strengthen that side of the primitive faith of Israel which already leaned in this direction. The settlement in Palestine, apart entirely from the appeal of the Canaanite cult, tended to strengthen this element in the life of the nation. How real the influence was can be gathered from a cult-hymn which Hosea quoted, as he had heard it chanted at an Israelite sanctuary.[1]

[1] Hosea vi. 1-3. I have seen no reason to withdraw the suggestion as to this origin for the hymn, which I first made in *Religion of Israel under the Kingdom*. The three verses have been made the theme of a hymn which appears among the Scottish Paraphrases. But my fellow-countrymen, many of whom are familiar with it, may recognise that the translator has supplied the element of an ethical and evangelical note, which Hosea missed. He has done to the hymn exactly what, in my judgment, the prophetic school did to the cult with which it was once connected.

In this Yahweh was invoked in terms which were suitable to a nature-god. His anger had been real and had troubled the people, but they counted it sure that this could not last, any more than the night or the winter can last. In three days at the utmost He will return with a healing as sure as the recurrent dawn or the spring rain. Therefore Hosea countered the cheap optimism of the people's reverence by a demand for repentance. Because Yahweh's anger was no casual thing like a summer drought, but had its source in His nature, it could only be satisfied, and He could only return on the condition of a change of heart in Israel. What one prophet aimed at effecting in connection with a cult-hymn, the religious leaders of the nation needed to effect over against the new danger which was threatening the cult. They must supply the rites which were growing up in the new conditions of Palestine with an ethical and spiritual content.

It ought perhaps to be insisted that no claim is made here as though the development of the festivals which has been sketched were proved. In the uncertainty of our knowledge and in the scantiness of our material for reaching a conclusion no such claim can be made. How much of festival ritual Israel brought with it to

Palestine, and what purpose it sought to effect by those rites, if it did practise them, we do not know. What we do know is that the religious leaders of the people supplied rubrics which were to be repeated in connection with the rites, either by the worshipper himself or by the officiating priests. In general these rubrics contain an ascription of the whole to Yahweh, adding briefly or at greater length a statement as to His nature, dwelling also on His peculiar relation to the worshipper or worshippers. They also stated the reason for and the purpose of the offering. The fact that it was recognised to be useful or necessary to accompany the outward rites of the cult with such rubrics is in itself significant. For it is the weakness of every cult-act that it is not self-explanatory, but may convey half a dozen meanings according to the mind of the worshipper who fulfils it. In order to recognise this we need only consider the position of the Christian Church in relation to the Holy Communion, its peculiar cult-act. Yet, although St Paul supplied a rubric which defined the purpose of the cult-act and its place in the Church's life, Christendom is to-day divided, not in the elements it employs for the celebration, but in the thoughts with which the worshippers approach their common and simple rite. Israel had the more need to define the sense which it attached to its rituals, because these, so far as their outward form was concerned, were not peculiar to itself, but closely resembled those of the surrounding nations.

The rubrics added by the religious leaders of the nation supplied precisely the distinctive element in the rites, by which they were distinguished from the similar customs of the rest of the world, for in these the men embodied their own thoughts about God, His nature, His relation to the worshippers, and the purpose of the offerings. A parallel may be drawn between their action and the attitude of the Presbyterian Communion, which has always held firmly by an approach to God ministered to men through word and sacrament, not through sacrament alone, nor through the word alone, but through the combination of the two.   The sacrament must have a specifically Christian intention, or it is empty : the word must issue in an act of worship, or it is incomplete.   The reasons which led the later Communion to insist on this attitude were wholly different from those which impelled the Hebrew priesthood to guard its cult from abuse : but the results show certain analogies.   It is profitable to examine a few illustrations of the combination of rubric and cult-act, of word and sacrament in early Israel, and to discover, so far as the facts make it possible, the aims which prompted its adoption.

There is, then, a simple ritual in connection with the offering of the first-fruits, which has been described in somewhat full detail.[1]   It has two parts : the outward form of the offering is described in vv. 1-4, 10 *b*, 11, the rubric which must accompany it is found in vv. 5-10 *a*.   As to the custom of offering these first-fruits, it must remain doubtful whether Israel practised such a rite before the settlement in Palestine. What is clear is that, even if it had, the custom must have received a much greater prominence after the change in the people's conditions of life after the conquest.   Harvest meant more to an agricultural community than it could have done in their wilderness life.   Whether, then, the custom was wholly new or merely of more signal importance, the need was felt to safeguard it from abuse through its similarity to heathen practice.   In order to show how this safeguard was supplied, I quote an incident in a very different field, which may at first appear very remote from the subject.   A missionary in Bechuanaland was consulted by a young chief who had recently succeeded to his father's

[1] Deut. xxvi. 1–11.

authority, and who had become a Christian. According to tribal custom, the young chief was required, at the season when his people began their spring ploughing, to perform in his official capacity a ritual, the purpose of which was to protect the grain against evil spirits and to guarantee its growth. The new chief was troubled as to what he ought to do. He had scruples about celebrating a pagan ritual, because it acknowledged the existence and the power of spirits in which he no longer believed, and because it was associated with incantations which were to him empty or even mischievous. So he consulted his friend the missionary as to what he ought to do ; and Mackenzie has described in his diary not only what he advised, but the thoughts which guided him in the advice he offered. He could not but recognise that the *letsemma* of the Bechuanas was a good thing, so far as its underlying conviction was concerned. For it implied the recognition, even the formal and public acknowledgment, that the life of the tribe depended on more than man's skill and diligence. What was false in it was the reference of any power to the evil spirits, with the consequent idea that all which was necessary for the tribe's well-being was to counteract their evil influence by certain spells.

H

So he prepared a form of religious service, such as could be used by a Christian, and the character of which may be found in his life by his son.[1] On the appointed morning young Khama went out with his plough and stated to the assembled tribe that he was about to perform his Christian *letsemma*. If, however, he added, any members of the tribe were dissatisfied and wanted more, they were at liberty to provide it for themselves by having recourse to the regular enchanters. The outward form of the rite was retained, but its meaning and its purpose were changed by the addition of a new rubric.

The task of the religious leaders in Israel was similar to that of Mackenzie in Bechuanaland : they had to superinduce on practices which were more or less pagan in their associations the convictions of an ethical and spiritual faith. To have broken entirely with the past would have meant to bewilder the minds of those who trusted them, and to lose the opportunity of preserving from that past what was worthy in

[1] *John Mackenzie*, by W. D. Mackenzie, 1902, pp. 143–45. It is interesting to notice that the leading features of this ritual were borrowed from the Psalter. In matters of this kind it is suggestive to recognise that Mackenzie had to turn to the Old Testament : he could not find guidance from the New. Again the cult of old Israel could supply guidance to Christian practice.

it. When now we turn to the Hebrew *letsemma* for the offering of first-fruits, there appear two leading characteristics, both of which reveal the means the men used for making the rite suggest to those who took part in it the convictions of their own faith. The first is stamped on the entire ritual. When the passage which describes it is read aloud, the first thing which must impress a listener is the constant iteration of the phrases Yahweh, Yahweh thy God, Yahweh my God, Yahweh our God. The repetition of the divine name sounds monotonous, even a little superfluous, when it is read in church or in a classroom. But the regulation was not intended for those conditions : its purpose was to guide the worship of Jewish peasant farmers who might have Canaanite neighbours practising a similar rite in honour of their own god. The significance of the reiteration of the name of the God of Israel is only seen when we recognise what it was meant to exclude : the first-fruits must be offered to Yahweh, not to baal. This underlying purpose becomes even more clear when we note the connection in which the divine name appears. The shrine to which the worshipper brought his offering must be one which Yahweh chose to set His name there, the priest who received it must be one who served the altar of Yahweh, the land from which the first-fruits came was the gift of Yahweh to the worshipper, and the offering itself derived from the bounty of Yahweh.

In its emphatic repudiation of any acknowledgment of baal, the ritual observance of first-fruits was in agreement with the first demand made on the people after the settlement. Israel was the people of Yahweh: as it owed everything, its existence as a nation, its possession of its land, the fruitfulness of that land, to the grace of its God, it must reserve its entire allegiance to Him. Therefore the cult, which expressed this allegiance and maintained the relation to Him, must be celebrated at altars of His appointment and according to the direction of His priests.[1]

Yet this did not fulfil the whole desire of the legislators, and does not exhaust the contents of the passage. The religious leaders of Israel were not satisfied with the merely negative result of avoiding any acknowledgment of a strange god. They included a positive element, in order that every worshipper, when he presented his first-fruits, might be reminded of the nature of Him to whom he gave them. The

[1] See, further, my *Code of Deuteronomy*, pp. 25 ff.

offering of the first-fruits must be an act of
faith in Israel's God, and must bring to the
worshipper a quickened sense of the character
of Him to whom it was rendered. Therefore
a rubric was added, which accompanied it on
every occasion : word and sacrament must go
together. The farmer was required to repeat a
form of words after the priest, at the time when
he deposited his offering before the altar. Again
it is necessary to think oneself back into the
conditions of the time, if one would appreciate
the meaning of the command. The men were
unlettered peasantry who possessed no prayer-
books, and who, or many of them, could not
have read them if they had possessed them.
The priest must, therefore, supply the form,
which the worshipper repeated after him. In
this rubric he had to state to whom he brought
his offering and what prompted his act. He
repeated that he was bringing his gift to Him
to whom he and his nation owed their possession
of the land in which he lived. While his fore-
father had been a wanderer from Aram, who
could call no place his own, he was settled
in a land which had been the gift of his God.
Without the help of God he should have had
nothing to bring. His first-fruits represented
his debt of gratitude to One to whom he owed

nationhood and land. When he accompanied the basket of his first-fruits with this prescribed formula, the worshipper did more than offer a gift to Yahweh at His appointed shrine and through His appointed priest. He made his act of faith in his own God, who had intervened in history to redeem Israel and to make it His people. Yahweh was no nature-god to whom the gifts of nature were naturally due : He was the God who controlled history in order to redeem Israel. Israel, therefore, brought its offering to One who meant well by it, and on whose assured purpose of grace it could continually depend.

The terms of this act of faith in the offering of first-fruits thus embodied the same convictions which dictated the changes in connection with Passover. In the one case, we have to do with a custom which was native to Israel : in the other, with a custom which may have sprung up after the conquest. The method of dealing with the two is not the same. But the effect in both cases was to transform the rite ; and in both cases the change was dictated by the ethical and spiritual content of the Mosaic reform. It is possible to carry the analogy a little further, and to suggest that in the offering of the first-fruits, as in Passover, one effect was to deliver the people from fear of the evil spirits. Unfortunately we do not know with any exactness the ideas which lay behind the first-fruits offering, as we know those which were the background to the original Passover. But the Bechuana rite at seed-time was intended to secure the safety of the newly-sown grain by incantations which counteracted the power of the demons ; and parallels to such a practice are common all over the world. It is, of course, always necessary to remember that analogies in this field of study do not constitute proof. All that it is legitimate to say is that, if the note of fear of the evil spirits attached to the original offering of the first-fruits, the fact would explain the note which dominated and dominates the Jewish ritual. The note which is struck there is one of gratitude. Israel owed everything to its God ; its existence as a nation was His gift, its land had been bestowed by Him, the fruitfulness of that land of which the first-fruits were evidence derived from Him. The people had no need to bribe or conjure the harvest of next year from One whose relation to them was assured by His own act. " Thou shalt set it down before the Lord thy God, and worship before the Lord thy God : and thou shalt rejoice in all the good which the Lord thy God hath given unto thee and unto thine house."

It is possible to trace the same influence at work in modifying the three festivals of the Jewish year. The reason for such modification was the same as that which has been recognised in the case of first-fruits. While Israel had brought the custom of pilgrimage to a common sanctuary with it from Horeb, that custom had been altered by the settlement. In the beginning it served, as has been suggested, to bring the loosely federated tribes to a species of Amphictyonic Council at a common centre, where their unity was maintained by an act of common worship to the God of the federation. But the sporadic character of the conquest and the gradual way in which it was effected made it impossible to find a common centre to which the tribes could resort. Since the older method of the Amphictyonic Council proved impracticable, and since the necessity for a centralised authority was urgent because of the pressure of the Philistines, the people turned to the expedient of the kingdom. One of the ends served by the festival at a central shrine was more effectively attained by the new institution.[1] But the old custom

[1] I have always felt that some explanation was needed for the strong opposition to the institution of the kingdom which appears in the record in the Book of Samuel. The reason cannot lie merely in the fact that the larger tribes, which had made good their footing in their territory, were unwilling to

persisted, though it had lost much of its former significance in the national life. The people continued to go on pilgrimage to the local shrines. The loss, however, of a *raison d'être*, based on the life peculiar to Israel, exposed the festivals to a new danger. They contracted more and more the influence of the new conditions among which the people were living, and were assimilated to the seasons of the agricultural year with an inevitable

lose their autonomy in the kingdom. It is, of course, true that the centrifugal tendency was present and broke out even under David. But there is no evidence for its presence in the records. On the contrary, the movement for a king to reign over them is always said to have found its origin and its support among the people. The opposition came from Samuel, the prophet and priest, and was based by him on religious grounds. He regarded the act of the people as nothing less than a rejection of Yahweh's rule over them. That attitude must imply more than a mere demand for the continuation of the conditions which prevailed in the period of the settlement, according to the editor of the Book of Judges. His view of the period, according to which Yahweh raised up a series of temporary rulers whose charismatic gifts were His direct endowment, is too theoretic in character to be other than a later attitude to events. It were more easy to understand the rôle assigned to Samuel if we could suppose that there existed then some institution based on religion which exercised a loose authority over the tribes, such as the Amphictyonic Council referred to. The institution of the kingdom would put an end to its authority for ruling, though not to its influence in religious matters. The new step might well appear to more conservative minds to be a refusal " to have Yahweh to rule over Israel."

drift towards the nature-religion of the new land.

The danger of all this movement did not escape the knowledge or the attention of Israel's religious leaders. In order to recognise this, it is only necessary to recall one fact, which is matter of common knowledge. At a later period Israel carefully associated the three leading festivals of its sacred year, not with the agricultural seasons, but with outstanding events in its national history. That is to say, it supplied a *raison d'être* for each of the rites, which was taken from its peculiar religion. Unleavened Bread was connected with the Exodus, Pentecost with the law-giving at Horeb, Tabernacles with the wilderness period. This process belonged to a much later period. Yet, while it has nothing to contribute directly to the earlier time, the question remains whether it was not the culmination of a method of dealing with the festivals which began much earlier. The very artificiality of the connection which is there instituted between Pentecost and the promulgation of the law may in itself suggest that the ingenuity of a later generation was there at work on the task of supplying something which was lacking in the case of this particular festival.

Is there any evidence for an earlier attempt having been made to institute a relation between the other two festivals and the events of Israel's history, which connoted the peculiar relation of Yahweh to the people? So far as Unleavened Bread is concerned, the combination of this festival with Passover certainly served that purpose, since Passover had been transformed into a celebration of the Exodus and made a commemoration of the divine deliverance then. Yet the date, when the single day of Passover was added to the seven days of Mazzoth, remains uncertain. It could not have been done so long as Passover continued to be celebrated in the homes of the people, and so must have followed the time when Passover was transferred to a sanctuary. Only then could the earlier rite have been combined with a festival at a shrine. If it were possible to determine the period in the national history at which Passover ceased to be a family rite, it would also be possible to see when and how Unleavened Bread came to be associated with the Exodus. But that question is bound up with the cognate one of how far Deuteronomy was revised in the interests of centralisation. In its festival calendar Deuteronomy ordered that the locus for Passover must be transferred to a sanctuary.

In the judgment of the majority of scholars that was a novel feature belonging to the period of Josiah's reform: until my volume on Deuteronomy has received a better answer than the obvious and inept remark that its position has not been accepted by the majority of scholars, I must remain convinced that it belonged to the unrevised code and considerably ante-dated Josiah's reform.

As for Tabernacles, it was evidently associated with the period of the wilderness life, for, when the practice of living in booths during the festival was adopted by the whole nation after the Return, it was stated that this was a custom of the earlier stage in the national life which had lapsed after the settlement.[1] In order to commend the use of these booths to that section of the nation to which it was novel, men felt it necessary to give this reason for its having fallen into abeyance for a period. The reason does not appear to a modern reader to be very convincing. According to its own traditions Israel had lived in tents during the years it spent in the wilderness, and it is not easy to see how the men could have obtained the material for the booths during those years. But the very

[1] Neh. viii. 13–17, cf. Lev. xxiii. 42, 43. On the question of booths at the festival, cf. my Post-Exilic Judaism, pp. 264 ff.

artificiality of the reason advanced only throws into stronger relief the close association which by that time had been established between Tabernacles and the wilderness period. The adoption of the practice of living in booths was made possible when it could be urged that thus the association of the cult-practice with the past of Israel's history was confirmed. The action taken after the Return was only the completion of a process which had begun long before.

A more direct and illuminating illustration of the way in which Tabernacles was supplied with motives taken from Israel's peculiar religion has been preserved in Psalm 81, the liturgy which accompanied the sacrifices at that festival in Northern Israel. It opens with an ascription of praise to Him in whose honour and after whose command the solemn feast-day rite was being celebrated. The psalm was chanted by a choir to the accompaniment of timbrel and harp, psaltery and trumpet. The service, both in itself and in its order, was a חק, or statute which belonged to Israel, a משפט, or ordinance of the God of Jacob, who appointed it for Joseph when He went out against the land of Egypt. The priests solemnly declared in the hearing of the worshippers that the rite which they were celebrating was wholly their own, following a ritual which was peculiar to themselves in honour of their own God and in memory of the deed He wrought when He redeemed the people. Suddenly, however, the note was changed, for the full-voiced choir gave place to a single voice, which spoke to the people in the name of the God who had redeemed them and had appointed their ordinance.

I removed his (*i.e.* Israel's) shoulder from the burden;
His hands were freed from the basket.
Thou calledst in trouble, and I delivered thee;
I answered thee in the secret place of thunder.
I proved thee at the waters of Meribah.
Hear, O my people, and I will testify unto thee:
O Israel, that thou mightest hearken unto Me:
There shall no strange god be in thee;
Neither shalt thou worship any strange god.
I am the Lord, thy God
Who brought thee up out of the land of Egypt;
Open thy mouth wide, and *I* will fill it.

In outward form and in content the verses form such an oracle as the prophets were in the habit of delivering. Thus the message is issued in the name and by the authority of God Himself. It is also based upon the revelation of His character which God made to Israel, and from that it develops the relation which has resulted between God and the nation. The difference

between the utterance in the Psalter and the
oracles in the prophetic books is due to the
different conditions in which they were spoken.
In the prophetic oracles the authors seized
upon some feature in the nature of Yahweh's
relation to Israel, set over against that the
actual condition of the people and denounced
the divine anger on their disobedience. Or
they reminded a discouraged people that the
relation between them and their God, because
it was based on the divine purpose with and
for them, could not be reversed by anything the
world might bring against them. The message
in the liturgy is another method of employing
the same great convictions. It supplied a
rubric to be used in connection with a cult-act
of Israel on its solemn feast-day. The purpose
of that act was to maintain the relation between
the nation and its God. Therefore the rubric
began by stating the act of the divine election
which had instituted this relation, and continued
by a reminder that the inevitable outcome of
such a relation was that Yahweh must receive
an absolute allegiance—there must be no strange
god in Israel. This rubric followed directly
on the choral ascription of praise to Him who
had instituted the rite and in whose honour
it was celebrated. Whether the rubric was

chanted by a leading priest or spoken by a
prophet, the single voice and the full choir
combined to insist on the fundamental demand
of Yahwism. He to whom Israel owed everything must alone be acknowledged by His
people, and He must be worshipped at His
own altars according to a ritual of His own
appointment. The worship offered to Him at
the festival must have associations with Him
only. Therefore all the motives in the liturgy
were derived, not from the association of Tabernacles with the harvest festival, but from the
national history and from the character of Him
without whom the people would have had no
history. The God whom Israel worshipped,
even at its nature-festivals, was different in
character from the nature-gods : the rite by
which Israel worshipped Him must quicken in
them the recollection that He was the God of
history and of redemption. One reference to
the other associations of the festival is found
in the last sentence of the rubric : " open thy
mouth wide and I will fill it." The God to
whom Israel owed its existence and its liberty
would not forget that the nation needed bread.

The analogy between this liturgy and the
law as to first-fruits is so obvious that it need not
be pursued. The reason for even mentioning it

is that the two cases illustrate the method taken by the priesthood for guiding humble men into a true understanding of their cult. They were not content to lodge their conception of God and His relation to men in a law which could form a manual for the guidance of their own practice, but which might never reach the common man. Every year, when the farmer brought the first-fruits of his harvest, he repeated sentences which clothed those great convictions in language that he could understand, language also which linked up his simple act with all the past of his nation. Every year, when the community closed their year with a harvest thanksgiving, they heard repeated the same convictions which gave Israel its unique place in its world, its identity, and its unity. In the same way the religious leaders of the nation were not content to forbid human sacrifice in a formal act of legislation : they clothed it in one of the most lovely and moving stories of literature. Men do not repeat the laws of a code : but mothers in Israel told the story of Isaac to their children, and the children did not forget.

In the liturgy of Tabernacles we find another instance of collaboration between priest and prophet in their common task of supplying

I

ethical and spiritual content to the national cult. The proof of such close collaboration would be strengthened if we could accept Gunkel's suggestion that it was an actual prophet who spoke the rubric in form of an oracle.[1]   Since, however, his proof involves a change in the text with no sufficient support from the versions, it is impossible to regard his conclusions as more than probable.   But, whoever spoke the verses, the combination of priestly practice and prophetic teaching is unmistakable, especially when closely similar procedure appears in the regulation about the first-fruits and the law of Passover.[2]

---

[1] *Cf.* his *Commentary on the Psalms*, ad loc.

[2] The appearance in Psalm 81 of a prophetic oracle in a rubric intended for the liturgical service at a festival calls up an interesting and suggestive feature in the chronicler's account of the arrangements made by David for the temple worship. According to him, 1 Chron. xxv. 1-6, certain guilds which claimed descent from Asaph, Heman, and Jeduthun were appointed to conduct the musical service.   Kittel, in his commentary on Chronicles, *ad loc.*, has pointed out that these men are not called levites, and that there is reason to believe that Asaph, at least, had originally no connection with this branch of the temple personnel.   That is a cautious understatement of the case, for the guilds of chapter xxv. are definitely separated from the levites, whose appointment is independently described in the opening verses of chapter xxiv.   Not only so, but the allocation of the two groups into courses is also described quite separately in the closing verses of the two chapters.   The two sets of clergy are distinguished.   Now, this difference between levite and singer goes along with a distinction in their functions, other than the fact that the singers supervised the

It would be possible to examine a number of psalms from this point of view, to show their liturgical character and their use in connection with the cult. Some, like Psalm 81, were intended for the worship of the community, and were chanted by the levitical choirs, which took so large a place in the services of the

music. For it was their task to prophesy with harps, psalteries, and cymbals, and Asaph is said to have prophesied beside the king, while Heman is called, " the king's seer in the divine words." The association there of certain cult-officials with prophecy in the fulfilment of their duties is too clear and too remarkable to be ignored. Nor does Kittel's suggestion that the intention was to magnify the office of the levites by ascribing to them prophetic powers meet the situation, for it fails to explain why these powers were confined to the singers who may not originally have been levites.

The questions which are there raised are too large to be discussed here. On the one hand, it is necessary to determine whether chapters xxiv. and xxv. are homogeneous ; and, if it should appear that they have been revised by a later hand, it is necessary to decide which sections in them derived from the original chronicler. On the other side, it is pertinent to examine the relation between these officials who prophesied in connection with their cult-duties, and the fact that the chronicler frequently and uniquely refers to levites who exercised the gift of prophecy. The reason for referring to the matter here is that this note may attract the attention of younger students. If they have not yet adopted, except for examination purposes, the orthodox view on the date and source of the Books of Chronicles in the official Introductions to the Old Testament, they may be willing to recognise that there is room, as there is need, for an unbiased study of the subject. Meantime the matter has a connection with the " cult-prophets " already mentioned on p. 75.

second temple. Others were meant for the use
of individuals, and were simpler, like the offering
of the first-fruits. Among the communal hymns
we find two associated with a sacrifice at the
opening and the close of a campaign.[1] Others
were associated with a day of confession and
fasting and need not have been accompanied by
a sacrifice.[2] Psalm 114 is a hymn for Passover,
which may have been chanted in the temple
when the lambs were slaughtered by the priests,
or sung in the home after the actual offering.
There is a considerable number of communal
thanksgivings which were suitable for the
festivals, or were used in connection with the
regular offerings such as the tamidh, in name
of the community.[3] In these, with the excep-
tion of the war-hymns, large use was made of
the events which accompanied and immediately
followed the Exodus. But the purpose of these
references to the national history was not to
glorify Israel; it was to insist on the peculiarly
close relation between Israel and its God. Sometimes the theme was the divine care over, at
others it was the divine patience with, the
people;[4] but always the psalmists dealt with the

[1] Psalms 20, 21.   [2] Psalms 80, 106, 44.
[3] Psalms 135, 136, 105.
[4] *Cf.* my *The Psalter in Life, Worship, and History*, Lecture II.

character of God. Again, we find cult-hymns
which were intended for the use of individuals.
Some of these, like the penitential psalms, accompanied sin-offerings, and largely consisted of ex-
pressions of penitence. Some were thanksgivings
for deliverance from sickness, and these were
associated with a תודה or sacrifice of praise.[1]
In other cases a man paid a vow which he had
made in a day of distress, and with his offering
brought his acknowledgment of the grace he had
received.[2] Here the worshipper addressed his
prayer to the God of Israel, acknowledged that
he owed his deliverance to Him, and sometimes declared that, even in hours of dire need,
he had sought no other help. The sacrifice,
whether it was the offering of an individual or
that of the community, was brought by men who
were members of the covenant with Israel. It
did not therefore create or renew the relation
between Israel and its God, since that was
wholly due to the divine act : it maintained
the initial relation through acts which God
Himself had ordained. The significance of the
cult, according to these hymns, rested, not on
the rite *per se*, but on the character of Him who
had commanded it and on the attitude of those
who fulfilled it.

[1] *Cf*. Psalm 116.   [2] Psalms 54, 61, 107.

But every student of the Psalter knows how difficult it is to reach definite conclusions as to the dates of the individual psalms. The criteria which are to hand are so ambiguous that only in a few cases can a decision claim to be more than tentative. Yet it is possible to venture one general statement on the subject. The recognition of the essentially conservative character of the movement which made the temple and the sacrificial system the centre of Jewish polity after the Return, cannot fail to influence the attitude taken to the Psalter. As it becomes more clear that the post-exilic community restored a sacrificial system which was essentially the practice of their fathers, it will become also clear that they continued liturgies which had formed part of the cult. When that day arrives much of the material in the Psalter will be re-studied with a more open mind to the possibility that it came into existence gradually, in close connection with the needs of the developing cult, and was not created by the men who built the second temple. Meantime, however, it would be idle to base conclusions as to the character of the liturgies on what could justly be called unproved assumptions as to their date. It must be sufficient to use material which is admittedly pre-exilic, and from it to recognise

the change, and the character of the change, which
was made in the cult-practice of old Israel.   In
the case of Passover we see a native and vener-
able ritual transformed, alike in its outward
form and its inward meaning, in order to adapt
it to become a means for maintaining the relation between the God of Israel and His people.
The offering of first-fruits and the Feast of
Tabernacles have been left, so far as is known,
unchanged in their form, and have certainly
maintained their connection with the nature
seasons.   But to each of these ceremonies a
rubric has been added, which had the same
purpose and the same effect as the deeper change
which was made in Passover.   Tabernacles was
a communal rite, the offering of first-fruits was
brought by an individual, Passover was at once
a family and a national ceremonial.   The cult
in all these separate forms was submitted to
revision in the same interest.   The evidence
which has been called comes from different
quarters, from a historical book, from a code
of law, and from a collection of liturgies.   They
agree in bearing the same testimony.   From an
early date rites which in other respects closely
resembled pagan practice were adapted in order
to convey the historical and redemptive character of Israel's religion.   Priest and prophet

collaborated to supply ethical and spiritual content to the national cult.

This rationalising, as it may not unjustly be termed, of the Hebrew cult led to one general result in the view taken of all sacrifice. These were all regarded as ordinances of the God of Israel, and their efficacy came more and more to be construed along the lines of His revealed character. Since He had revealed Himself as the maker and redeemer of His people, the sacrifices He claimed could not be intended to cajole Him or to win a favour which He might otherwise have withheld. Israel believed that it knew the purpose of its God toward it, because it believed that He had made it known. Its sacrifices, which He had ordained, could have no effect in changing His immutable mind. Nor did these serve to initiate a relation between the people and their God : He had instituted this covenant relation. The purpose of their cult was to acknowledge what He had done for them and to maintain that which they had received. It became a grateful recognition of what He was. Now, to set the sacrificial system under the control of one leading idea was in itself a great step in advance. So far as it is possible to trace the primitive Hebrew rituals, these show the same confusion of thought about the relation between God and man, and therefore about the purpose and the effect of the sacrifices which embody that relation, as appears in the other ethnic religions. As has already been pointed out, the presence-bread was probably the last remnant of a feast intended for divine food. Again, the שלמים, or "peace-offerings," find their most natural explanation along the lines suggested by W. R. Smith[1]: they formed a communion feast in which god and worshippers had their share. When, as Buchanan Gray has pointed out,[2] Israel brought its sacrifices under one dominant idea, the result was to simplify and unify the whole system.

To deny any such unity of conception to the primitive Hebrew rituals, as well as to those of the other ethnic faiths, is to run counter to an influential school of opinion on the subject. An attitude similar to that of W. R. Smith has appeared in a more recent volume[3]: only where W. R. Smith believed it possible to find

---

[1] *The Religion of the Semites.* Smith's mistake appears to me to have been that he forced an explanation which was true of one form of sacrifice on all the others. Yet the existence of the presence-bread, a food in which the god alone shared, must warn against that ready solution.

[2] *Sacrifice in the Old Testament.*

[3] *Origins of Sacrifice*, E. O. James.

a common idea as to sacrifice in the Semitic world, Professor James claims to have discovered the basal conception which underlies all sacrifice. Again, a number of writers have combined to present the common cult-pattern which appears in several of the early peoples in the Near East, and to deduce from this a common conviction.[1] The results presented are very suggestive and brilliant, more brilliant, perhaps, than convincing. W. R. Smith found the clue to Semitic sacrifice in an ill-attested rite of an obscure Saracenic sept. Professor James discovered the key to all sacrifice in the cult of Mexico, of which, since no evidence for its meaning has survived, he has supplied the interpretation. The authors of the other volumes have selected analogies from most varied sources and combined them into a pattern, but leave the uneasy impression that they have ignored the differences. But all these scholars appear to hold one common preconception — that the mind of primitive man in dealing with religion was simple and even logical. Is not the opposite rather the truth? The mind of primitive man, instead of being dominated by one clear idea, is capable of harbouring entirely contradictory ideas on subjects to which he directs his

[1] *Myth and Ritual* and *The Labyrinth*.

attention. Nowhere is this truth more evident than in relation to religion. Even men who are far from primitive show themselves clear and keen when they deal with practical issues in life, but they hold quite incompatible ideas on a subject like religion. Instead of being the original possession of any race, simplicity of thought is the fine flower of severe self-discipline. Indeed we may measure the worth of any system or of any thinker by the extent to which it or he has succeeded in reaching it.

The fact, therefore, that Israel learned to construe its sacrifices in the light of one controlling idea is the proof that its priests were guided by a conviction which was not native to the cult itself, since that was compact of varied aims and ideals, but which reached them from another source and by a different means. It came from the revelation which was mediated through Moses at Horeb, a revelation which was the nerve of all the prophetic activity. But, as Buchanan Gray has further pointed out, the common idea which thus controlled the system of sacrifices was that of a gift. Dr Gray, in his study of Old Testament sacrifice, was seeking primarily to explore the evidence of the Hebrew documents and history, and he confined himself to his theme. Whatever resemblances might have once existed between their rituals and those of other nations, he proved that, from the time when the nation emerged into the light of history, sacrifice to it was either an act of homage from the inferior to his superior, or was intended to show gratitude to One from whom the worshipper had received some benefit. Whatever Israel brought to God was the expression of its dependence on Him, and the rubrics which accompanied its offerings dwelt on the fact. Sacrifice was not intended or needed in order to make God gracious ; it was brought in recognition of a grace which He Himself had assured. Even piacular sacrifice was construed from this point of view, and freed from the idea of its being valid for propitiation. The idea of man being able through the death of a victim, or through some act of self-immolation, to appease the anger of an offended deity or to change his mind toward the worshipper, has clung persistently in most religions to this form of offering. How alien it was to the Hebrew conception of the relation between God and man is clear from a statement in Leviticus xvii. 11, " For the life of the flesh is in the blood : and I have given it to you upon the altar to make an atonement for your souls." The fact that this remark is not set by itself, but occurs almost casually in connection with another subject, only makes it more significant. The writer who set it there did not need to isolate it for emphasis ; he could take it for granted that every reader would recognise its truth. Whatever purpose the blood of the victim served at the altar, it did not avail to make Yahweh gracious, for He against whom the offence had been committed had provided the means of atonement.

When the sacrificial system was thus brought under one controlling conviction, the basis of it all rested on the idea of the covenant at Horeb. God had delivered Israel, and had made it His people. The relation between Israel and Him was of His institution, and for any breach of that relation on the part of the people He had provided. The national cult served to maintain this initial relation : it could not cajole or bribe or threaten the deity.[1]

[1] It may help to avoid misunderstanding or even misrepresentation of this position to add that certain elements of cruder type persisted. The use of the ashes of a red heifer, Num. xix., and the ordeal for a woman suspected of adultery, Num. v. 5–31, are outstanding illustrations of the retention of magical practices. The priesthood seems to have been content to remove from these their association with another god, notably in the case of the red heifer, but otherwise to have left them alone. Both cases, however, formed no integral part of the regular cult, but were employed to meet special contingencies. Accordingly, they quietly disappeared in the course of time out of the life of the temple, as the elaborate

It is possible now to go back to the question which was raised at the beginning of this discussion and to see whether we are in a better position to answer it.   Judaism after the Return constituted itself round the temple and the sacrificial system.   Having lost everything else which gave them a centre and a rallying point, the men found both in their national cult. When Jewry took this step, the effect was to set a deeper gulf of separation between themselves and the world.   Most students of the national history will acknowledge that by this act the people lost a rich and valuable element in the prophetic teaching.   By insisting on the retention of the feature in their religion which was national and even local in its character, they certainly escaped the danger of absorption into an alien world.   But another element of their

regulations for levirate marriage disappeared out of the people's civil life.   They had ceased to fulfil any real function, except that of exercising the ingenuity of fundamentalist Rabbis.

In another more grave direction, however, Judaism never broke with an inheritance from its old cult, since it retained the idea of ceremonial uncleanness, and never recognised its radical incompatibility with an ethical and spiritual relation to God.   But it is useless to repeat what I have tried to say on that subject in *Post-Exilic Judaism*, pp. 299 ff.   I have also an uneasy conviction that all Christendom has not seen the full bearing of its Master's judgment with the same clearness as Augustine showed when he declared that there is no evil in things, there is only evil in the use men make of things.

faith, its universal character, which sprang directly from the ethical passion of the prophets, was inevitably obscured. From the time of the Return the Jew held two convictions which could not be finally reconciled. He believed that Yahweh, the God of Israel, was the God of the whole world; but he also believed that the worship of this God could only be fully maintained through rites which were the prerogative of one nation, and were legitimately celebrated at a single sanctuary.

Post-exilic Judaism was essentially a compromise, and to this extent it definitely turned its back upon the full message of its prophets. There is room for speculation as to whether, in the circumstances in which they and their world stood, the men could have done other than they did. There is also an opportunity to insist that in their conservative timidity they lost the chance to set before the world a religion of purely spiritual and ethical content. History, whether it deals with the outward affairs of the nations or with their inward convictions, is always presenting great opportunities to those who delight in being wise after the event. But fortunately the immediate concern of this study is the humbler task of discovering what the men of the Return did do and the relation of their act to the past of the nation. By the course which they chose did the men elect to follow a cult which was not native to their life, but which, alike in its origin and in its implications, was heathen? Did they therefore reject the entire message of their prophets, who had condemned this cult *per se*? Did the work of the men of the Return issue in no real compromise, but in a deliberate return to an element in their earlier faith, against which the finer spirits of the nation had unanimously and constantly protested? Such a position, as has already been said, fails to explain why a Judaism which had rallied round a system which was not native to its own genius, became through the act more conscious of itself as a teacher of the nations. It can as little show reason for the tough endurance of such a Judaism in an alien world, as it can account for its becoming the seed-bed for a faith which restored the forgotten elements after the Return, the ethical and spiritual and universal heritage of the prophets.

The contention of this discussion is that Israel brought with it out of the desert a cult which was its own, but which, because it antedated the Exodus and the Mosaic reform, represented a lower stage of religious development and was not essentially different from those of other nature-religions. The danger was real that the influence of the new conditions of their life and the influence of the example of their heathen neighbours might combine to assimilate the religious practices of the people to those of their environment. The effect would have been to nullify to all intents and purposes the advance in religion which had been gained at Horeb. The reform movement under Moses would have been reduced to a few theoretic propositions which were held *in vacuo*, but which had no direct influence on the rites the people performed in order to maintain their relation to their God. A reform which is confined to words can never remould the life of a nation. Priest and prophet united to meet this danger. Their first step was to forbid the use of all foreign emblems and of every foreign shrine. Yahweh must be worshipped at His own sanctuaries, through the agency of His own priests and according to His own rituals. This was comparatively easy, since it appealed to the pride of the conquerors, and was supported by the people's devotion to their familiar religious practices. As it was easier, it was more successful.

The more difficult, but an equally necessary, step was to reform those ancestral and beloved

K

rites in the light of the Mosaic convictions as to
the nature and character of Israel's God.   These
practices were not merely familiar, but they had
woven themselves into the very warp and woof
of the national life to an extent which it is hard
for the modern world to realise.   The process
of change must be slow and gradual : and it is
natural that the men whose charge it was should
not always have been in agreement on the rate
of change, on its extent, or on the method of
carrying it out.   There is evidence of a certain
tension between priest and prophet on these
questions, as there always has been between the
men who formulate a policy of reform and those
whose business it is to deal with the tough facts
of an actual situation.   The reformer has often
found it hard to be patient with the practical
politician, nor has the practical politician always
been sufficiently grateful to the gadfly who
stings him on by the fretting venom of an ideal.
But it has been possible to trace the steady
impact of one ideal, consistently urged by the
prophets on the cult of Israel, and to recognise
the varied methods by which this was made a
more worthy means of maintaining the nation's
relation to its God.   The result was that, when
Judaism constituted itself on the basis of the
cult, it rallied on something which was its own,

so native to its own genius that from this time it became more conscious of its distinctive character in an alien world. Yet the cult was not the system which the people had brought with them into Palestine. It had been transformed by what some prefer to call the prophetic ideal, what I prefer to call the convictions in the Mosaic reform. The result was a compromise, like everything else which men set up in this world, but through it the enriched and purified cult was able to shelter and to transmit the ideals of prophets and saints so that they became a ferment in later generations.

To construe the work of prophet and priest in old Israel along these lines restores to the religious history of the nation a real evolution. Otherwise the prophets are cut away from their roots in the life of their people. They emerge there, sporadic and isolated figures, bearers of a message which was peculiar to themselves and which they had discovered in solitude by means which were wholly their own. Naturally, when they are so conceived, the ecstatic character of their visions and auditions must be pressed in order to explain how they arrived at convictions so remote from those of common men. The message they brought was unwelcome, and, as it was unacceptable, it was ignored. They were, in other than the physical sense, voices crying in the wilderness, which failed even to produce an echo.   For they effected nothing of that which they attempted.   They condemned the means by which their people were seeking to worship and serve their God, but in the end of the day the people whom they had addressed constituted their new polity round the cult which they had unanimously rejected.   There was no development in Israel's religious life, because Israel refused to listen.

In reality the prophets sprang from the life of the nation, and had their roots deep in its past.   They were continually recalling their hearers to the memory of events which both interpreted alike, and of convictions which were the common property of all Israel.   Because of this, they never failed to find an audience, and an audience which preserved their oracles and used them as sources of religious guidance and inspiration.   They believed that they were in direct relation to God, but the God whose voice they heard was the God who had spoken to all Israel.   If they had anything to say, it was because God had chosen Israel to be the sphere of His self-revelation ; and, if their message disagreed with the initial revelation which He had made through Moses, it ought to be ignored. They were at once the most individual voices which ever spoke to men, and the steadfast upholders of a tradition. What they did was to draw conclusions as to right conduct, and as to methods of worship, from those facets of truth which seemed in danger of being forgotten. Therefore they did not always agree in the conclusions which they drew, but sometimes were found in opposition, not only to the multitude, but to one another. Because they always appealed to convictions which were common to them and their hearers, they could not expect to be accepted on their bare word and on their claim to have heard the authentic voice of God. Themselves the severest critics of their time in the light of these common convictions, they could not claim to be exempt from criticism in their turn. Their message must be pondered and even weighed. Men who worked along these lines were not creating a new thing, and they, who constantly appealed to the past, never supposed that they were. For these reasons their work did not pass away like a summer cloud. It did not effect all which the men hoped or desired. But it is not given to any of the children of men to realise all his desire, and it is not good necessarily that even a prophet should get all he wants. No one man has all the truth. But they contributed their amazing share to the task of remoulding the religion of their people, which was embodied in their cult. Because the cult of Israel was saturated through and through with the convictions of the prophets, because it had not merely been transformed through these, but was accompanied by rubrics which were Mosaic in their spirit, it was able to survive, while the cults of Assyria and Babylonia must be pieced together from the evidence of texts buried in the ruins of temples, the worship in which these once guided. Not only did it maintain itself, but it sustained the nation and prevented it from being absorbed as Assyria and Babylonia were absorbed. It was able to preserve in the minds of humble men the sense of a God who was different from the many gods of the heathen, and who was chiefly different in this, that He cared for more than a correctly offered and rich cult. He was One who was self-revealing and who in His self-revelation had shown His will to redeem His people. Because revelation was never static in Israel, because evolution or progress was essential to its conception of religion, it could not come to an end when Post-Exilic Judaism set up its new polity and made the law binding on its nation. In the fulness of time there was born to an Israel which worshipped God after the way of its fathers, One who was the self-revelation of the same God, a light to lighten the Gentiles as well as the glory of His own people, Israel.

INDEX OF SCRIPTURE REFERENCES

GENERAL INDEX

A

Abomination, 70, 83, 85, 86
Abraham, 12, 78 f.
Ahab, 75
Ahaz, 79
Alt, Prof., 6
altar, 17, 39, 40, 42, 64, 71,
    83, 91, 104, 116, 128, 140,
    141
Amos, 55, 66
"Amphictyonic Council,"
    105, 120
antinomy in early Judaism,
    51, 69, 72, 143
apostles, 50
Aram, 117
Asaph, 130
Asher, 86
Asherah, 12, 64
Assyria, 150
Atonement, Day of, 100
Augustine, 142

B

Baal, baalim, 58, 59, 64,
    115 *f.*
Babylonia, Babylonians, 23,
    32, 48, 95, 99, 150
baldness on the forehead, 64
baptism, 49

Barak, 56
Bechuanaland, 112 f., 119
Book of the Covenant, 6
Booths, 124
bread of presence, 98, 102,
    124, 137

C

Canaan, Canaanite worship,
    12, 16, 29, 39, 52, 53, 55,
    57, 58, 64 f., 78, 79 *n*., 83,
    86, 106, 108, 115
ceremonial demands, 21, 26,
    99, 142
Christ, 26, 49 f., 92, 142;
    Christian Church, Chris-
    tendom, 5, 26 f., 30, 48 f.,
    92, 110 f., 113 f., 142;
    Christmas, 92
Chronicler, 130
Circumcision, 50
Covenant, 41, 51; Book
    of, 6; at Horeb, 41, 44 f.,
    47, 65, 133, 136, 144
cult: origin of, 12 ff., 18 f.,
    29, 52 ff., 144; before
    the Exodus, 37 ff., 53 f.
    (Deuteronomy); early
    centres, 12, 16 f.; after
    conquest, 55 ff., 108 f.;
    purpose of, 136 ff.; de-
    termined by character of

Printed by
Turnbull & Spears, Edinburgh